TAYLOR SWIFT
reputation

ISBN 978-1-5400-2084-0

HAL•LEONARD®

7777 W. BLUEMOUND RD. P.O. BOX 13819 MILWAUKEE, WI 53213

In Australia Contact:
Hal Leonard Australia Pty. Ltd.
4 Lentara Court
Cheltenham, Victoria, 3192 Australia
Email: ausadmin@halleonard.com.au

Visit Hal Leonard Online at
www.halleonard.com

...READY FOR IT?

Words and Music by TAYLOR SWIFT,
MAX MARTIN, SHELLBACK
and ALI PAYAMI

Heavy Pop beat, in 2

ran - som.   Some,   some boys are try-ing   too hard.   He don't try at
is - land.   And,   and he can be my   jail - er,   Bur-ton to this

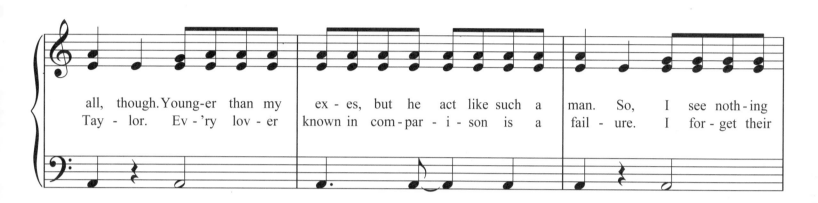

all, though. Young-er than my   ex - es, but he act like such a   man. So, I see noth-ing
Tay - lor.   Ev -'ry lov - er   known in com-par-i-son is a   fail - ure. I for-get their

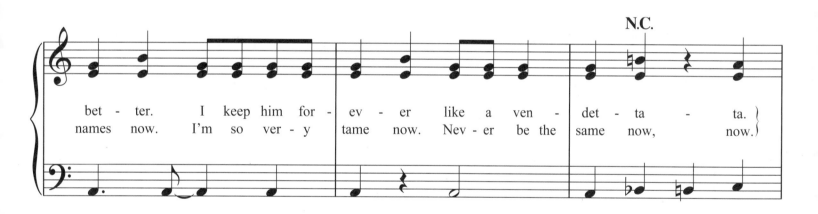

bet - ter. I keep him for - ev - er   like a ven - det - ta - ta.
names now. I'm so ver - y   tame now. Nev - er be the same now,   now.

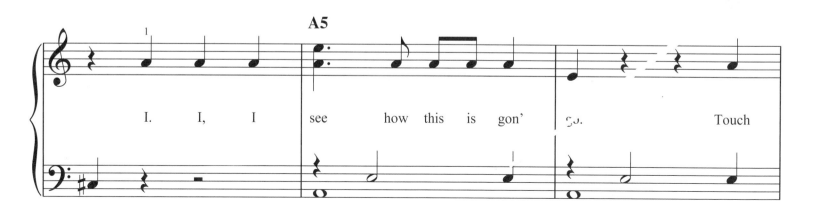

I. I, I   see   how this is gon' go.   Touch

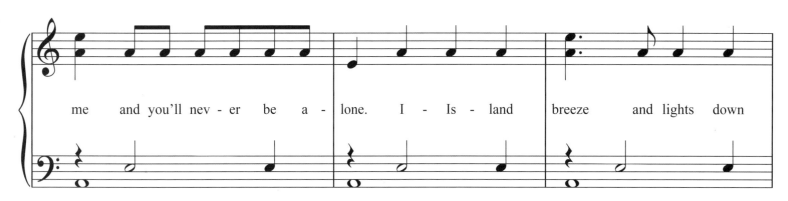

me and you'll nev-er be a-lone. I - Is-land breeze and lights down

low, no one has to know.___ In the mid-dle of the

night, in my dreams,___ you should see the things we

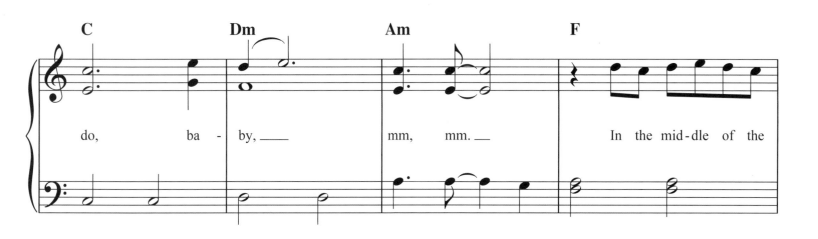

do, ba-by,___ mm, mm.___ In the mid-dle of the

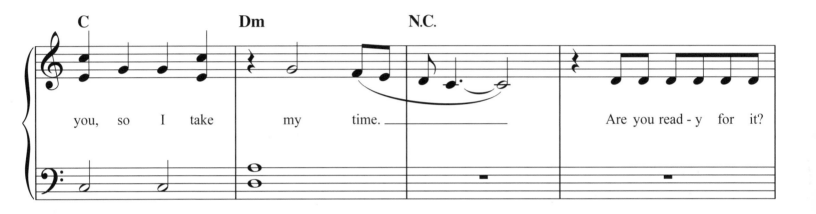

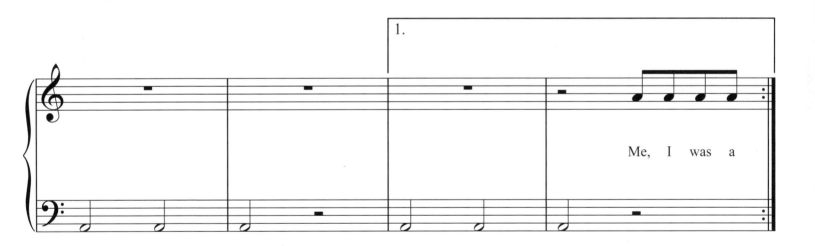

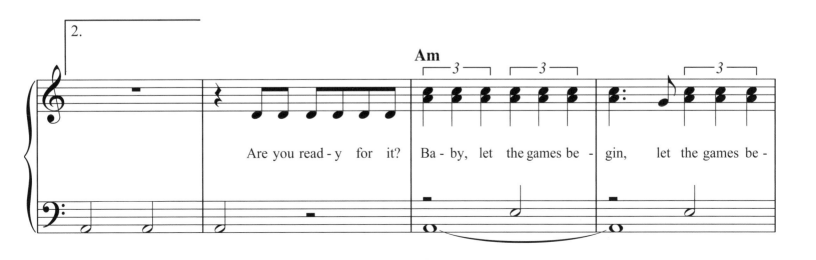

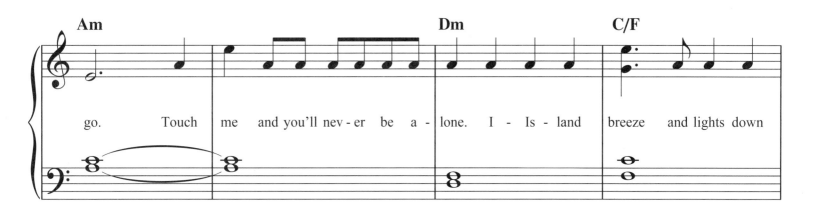

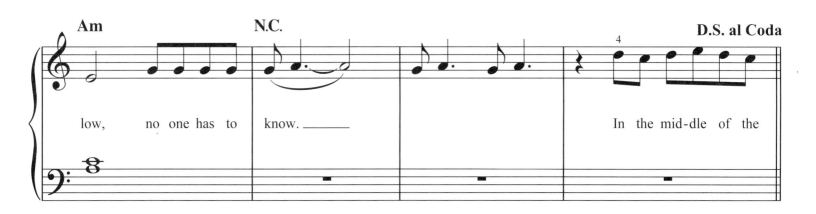

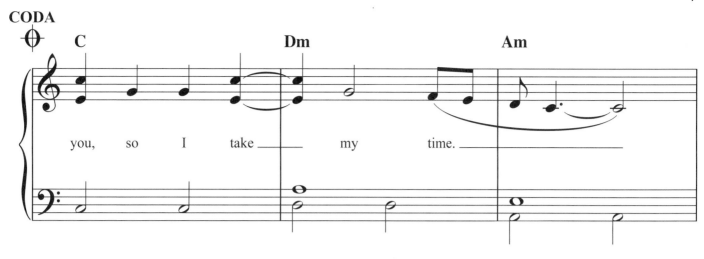

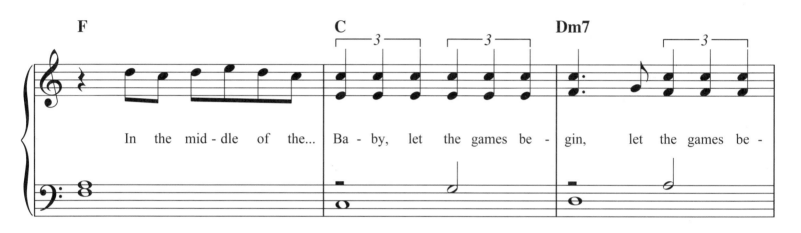

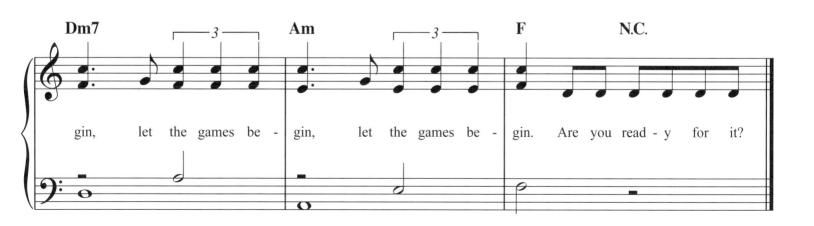

END GAME

Words and Music by TAYLOR SWIFT,
ED SHEERAN, MAX MARTIN,
SHELLBACK and NAYVADIUS WILBURN

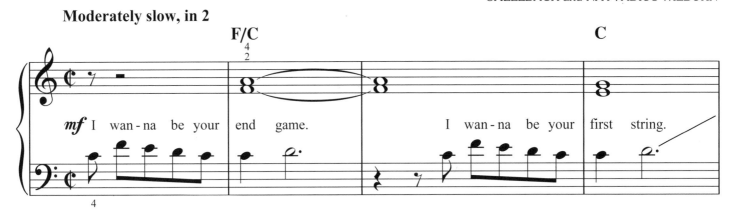

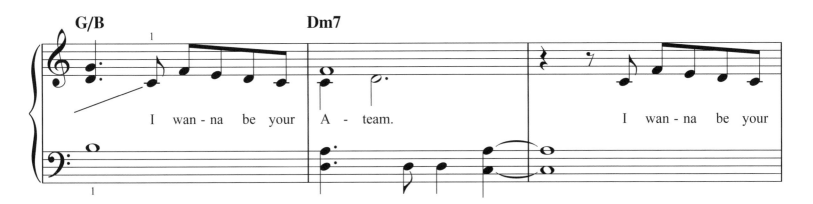

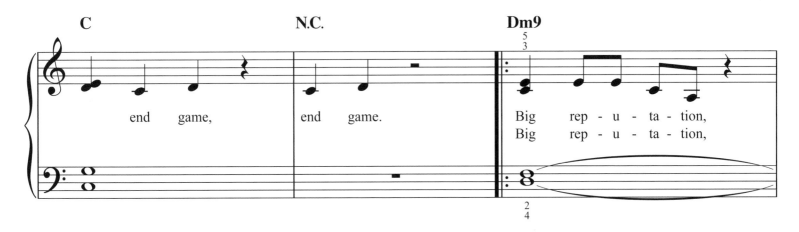

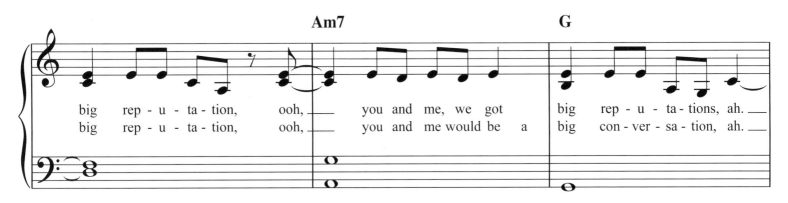

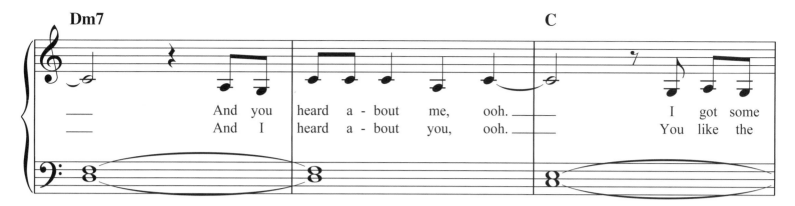

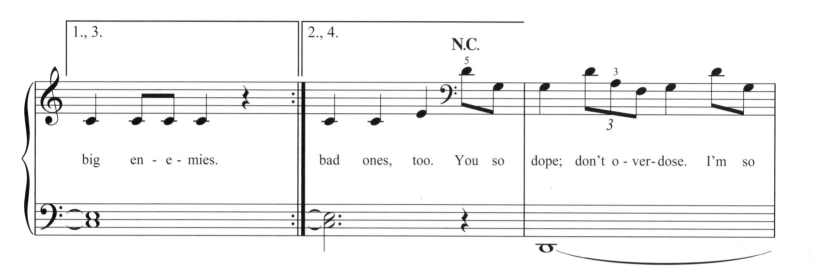

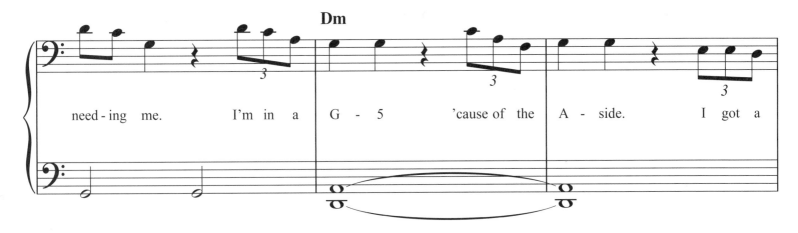

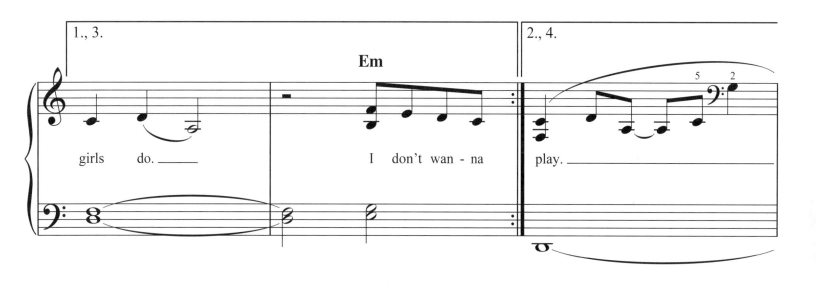

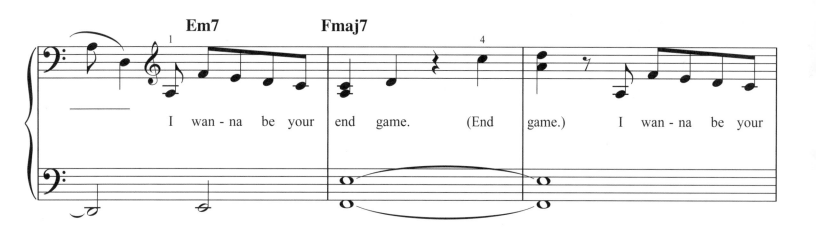

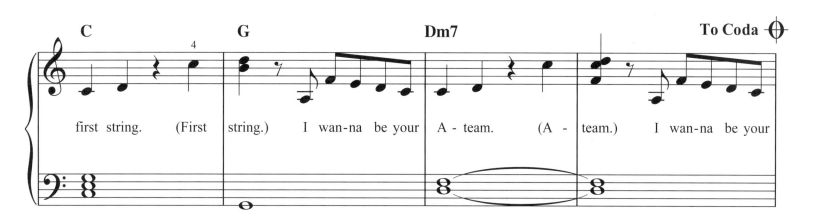

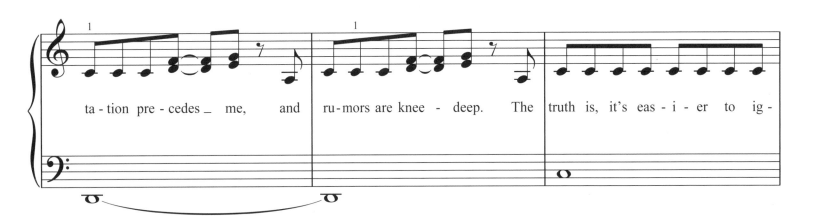

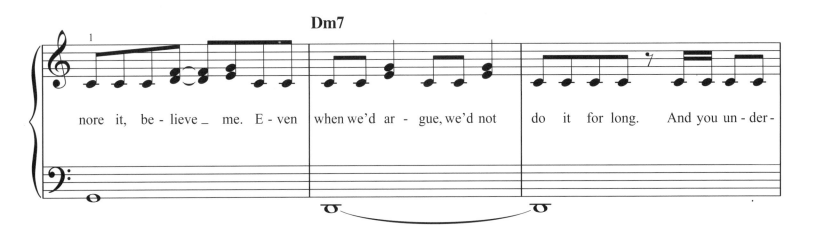

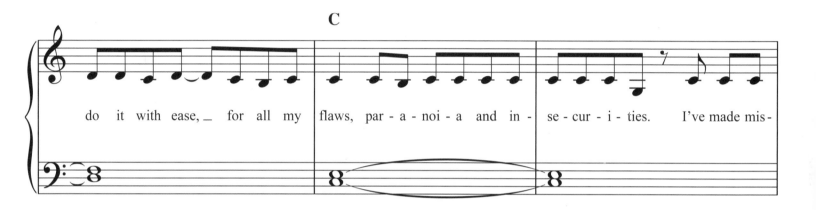

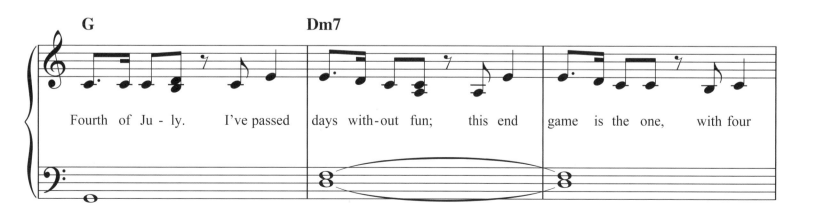

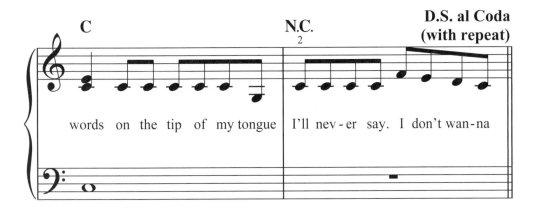

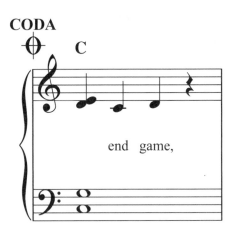

words on the tip of my tongue I'll nev-er say. I don't wan-na

end game,

end game.

Big rep - u - ta - tion, big rep - u - ta - tion, ooh, __
Big rep - u - ta - tion, big rep - u - ta - tion, ooh, __

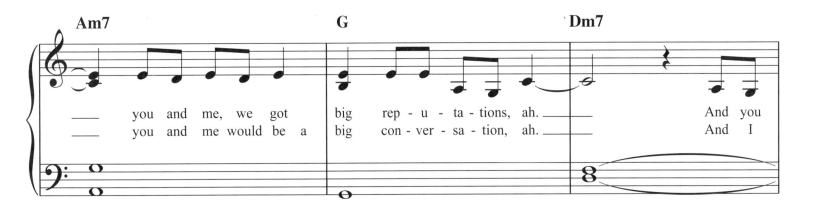

__ you and me, we got big rep - u - ta - tions, ah. __ And you
__ you and me would be a big con - ver - sa - tion, ah. __ And I

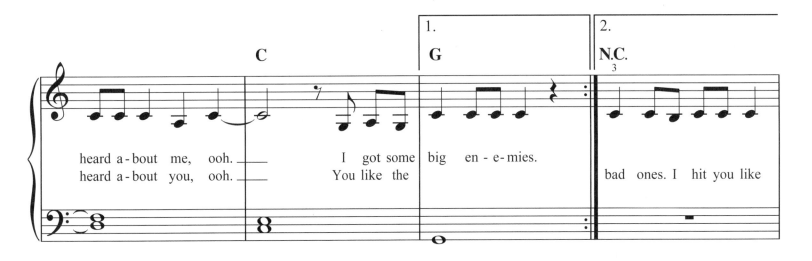

heard a - bout me, ooh. __ I got some big en - e - mies.
heard a - bout you, ooh. __ You like the

bad ones. I hit you like

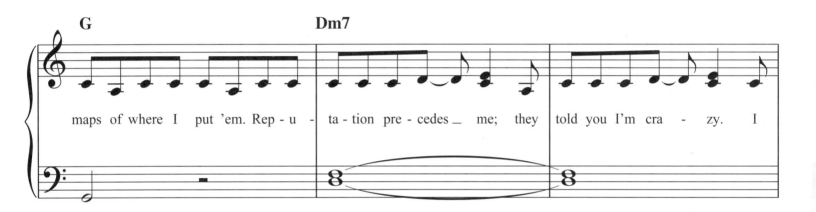

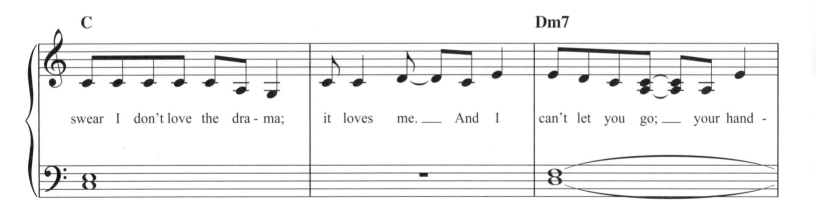

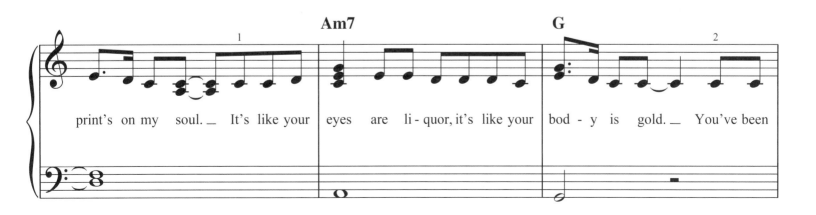

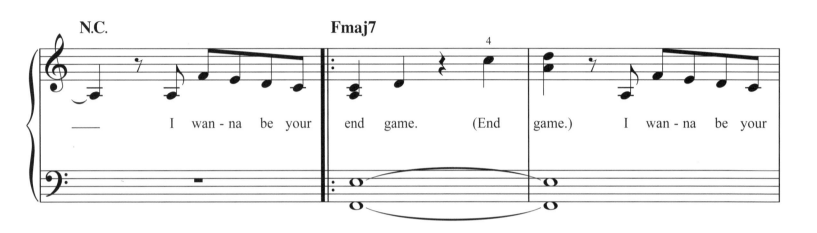

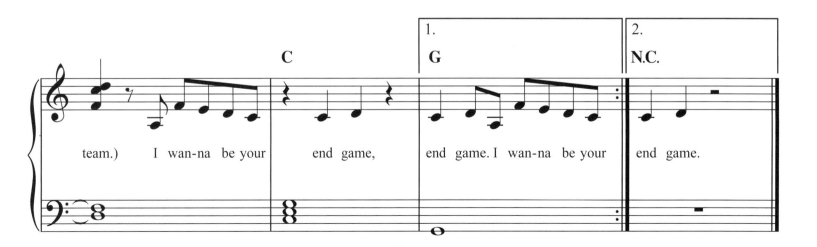

I DID SOMETHING BAD

Words and Music by TAYLOR SWIFT,
MAX MARTIN and SHELLBACK

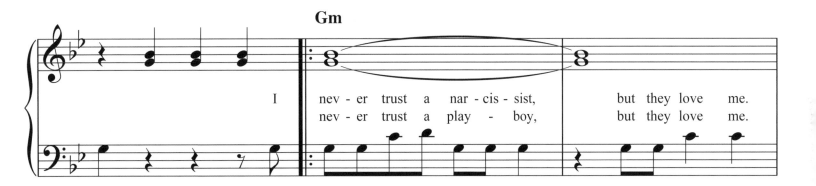

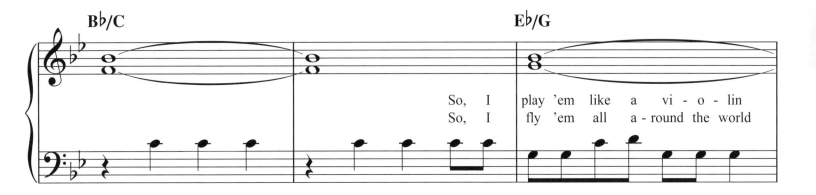

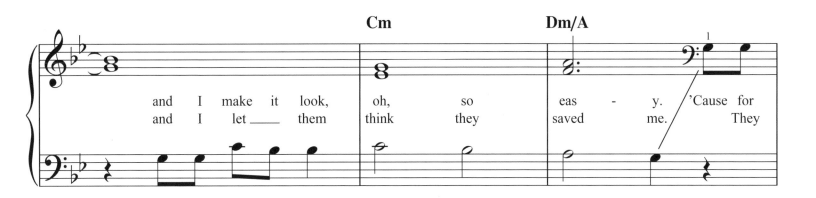

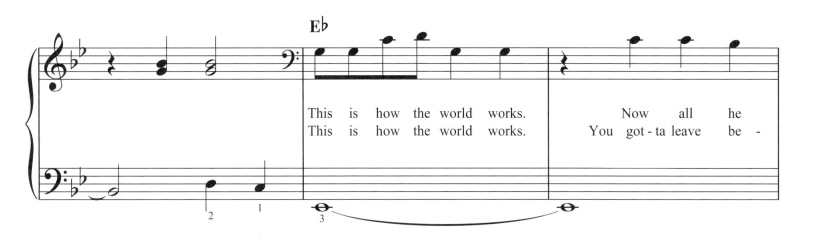

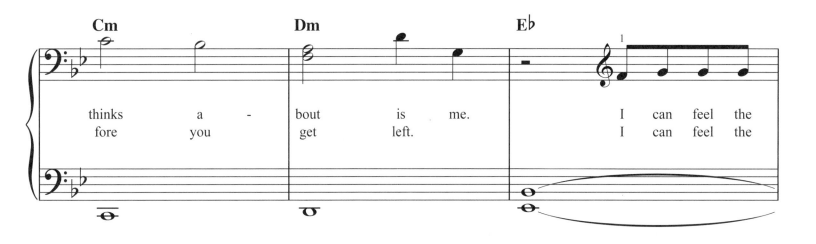

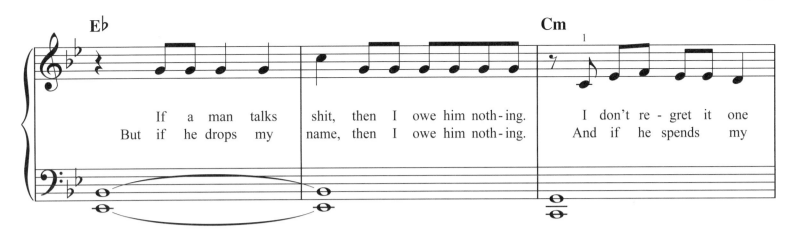

If a man talks shit, then I owe him noth-ing.
But if he drops my name, then I owe him noth-ing.
I don't re-gret it one

bit, 'cause he had it com-in'.
change, then he had it com-in'.

They say I did some-thing bad. ___ Then

why's it feel so good? ___

They say I did some-thing bad. ___

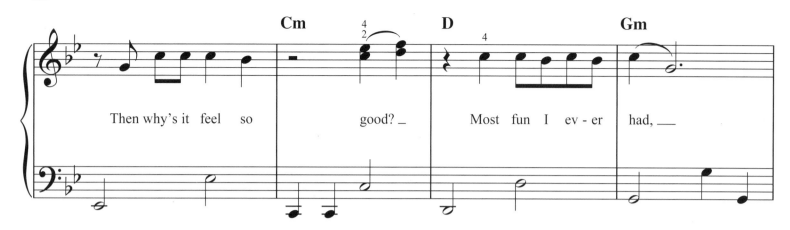

Then why's it feel so good? ___ Most fun I ev - er had, ___

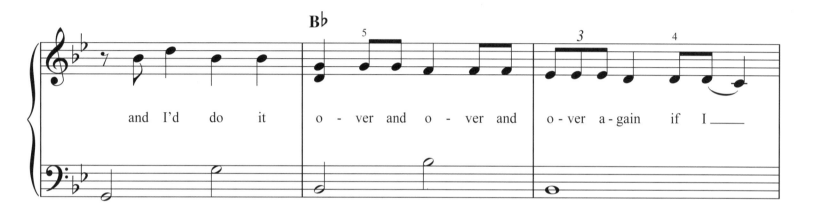

and I'd do it o - ver and o - ver and o - ver a - gain if I ___

could. It just felt so good, ___ good. ___

21

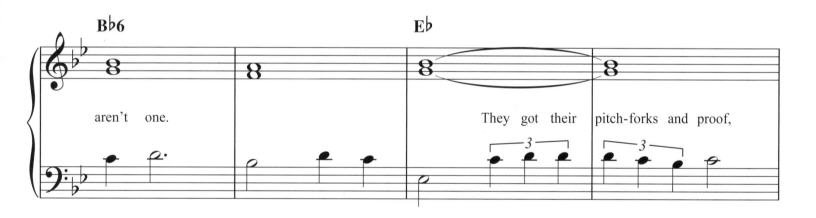

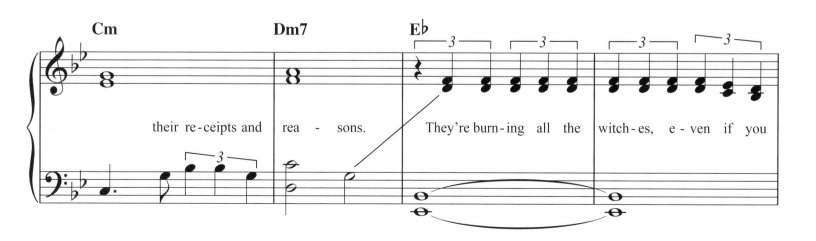

aren't one.   So, light me up,   light me up,

light me up. Go a - head and light me up,   light me up,

light me up,   light me up,   light me up.

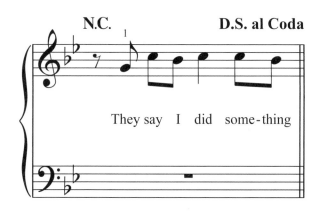

They say I did some-thing

Oh, _____ they say I did some-thing bad. _____

Why's it feel so good, _____ good? _____ So good,

why's it feel so good? Why's it feel, why's it feel so _____ good?

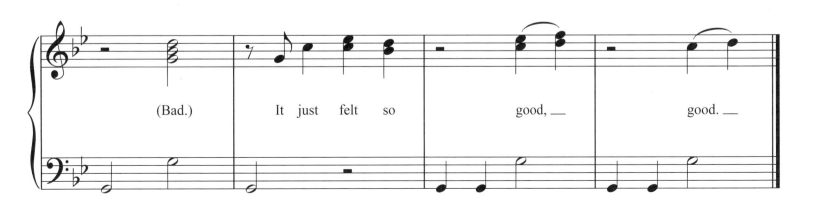

(Bad.) It just felt so good, _____ good. _____

DON'T BLAME ME

Words and Music by TAYLOR SWIFT,
MAX MARTIN and SHELLBACK

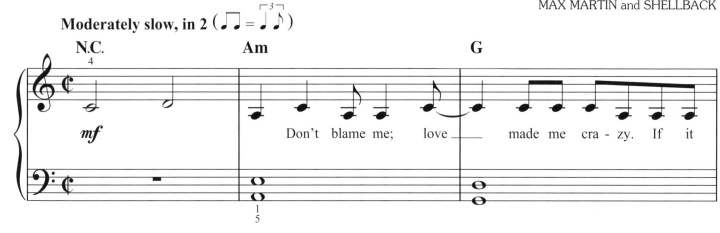

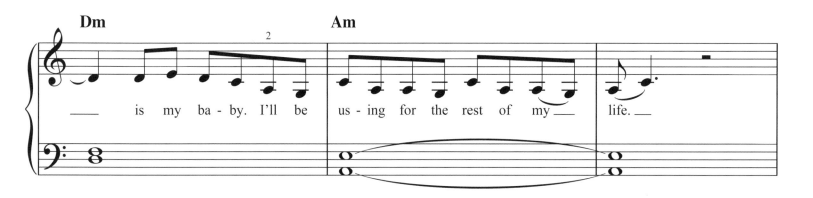

25

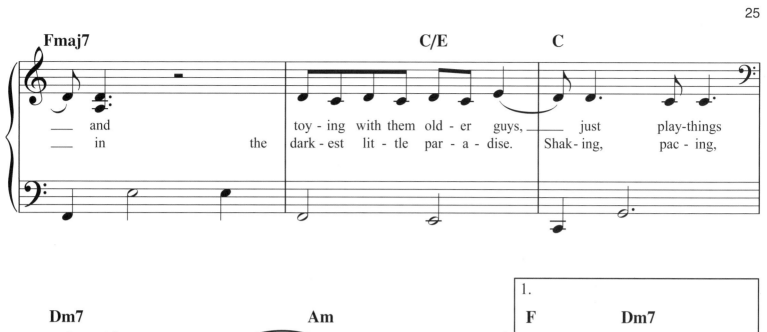

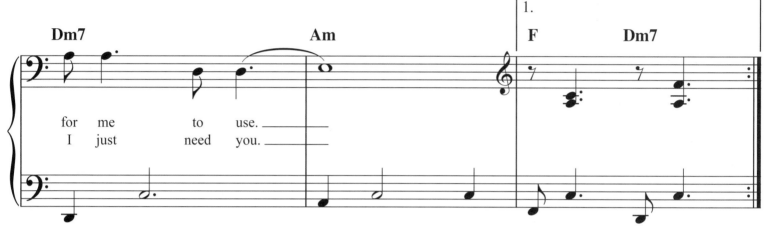

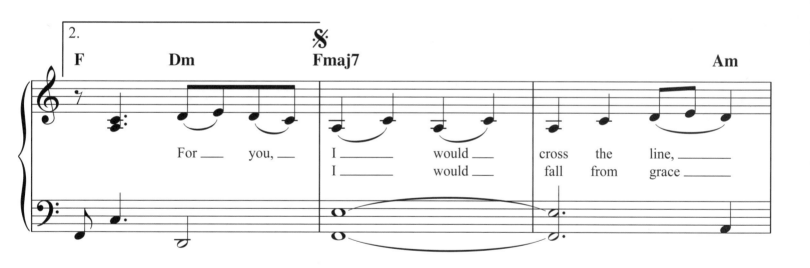

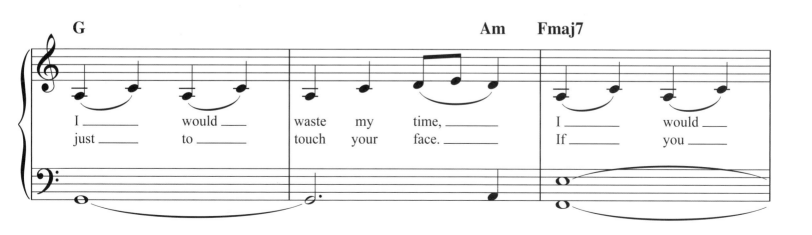

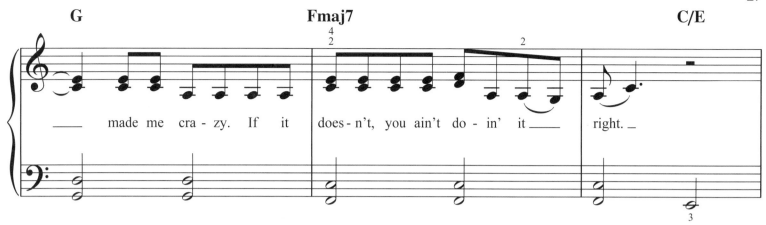

made me cra - zy. If it doesn't, you ain't do - in' it right.

Lord, save me; my drug is my ba - by. I'll be us - ing for the rest of my

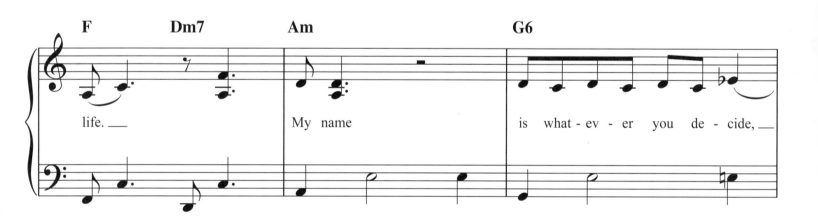

life. My name is what - ev - er you de - cide,

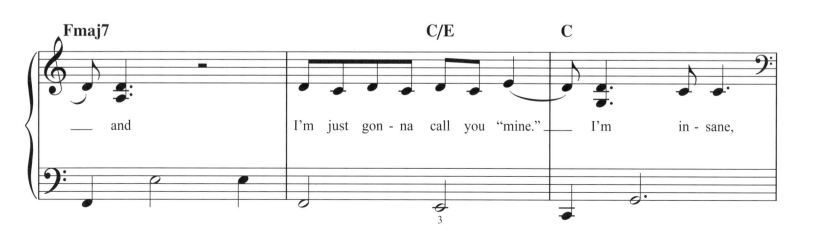

and I'm just gon - na call you "mine." I'm in - sane,

but I'm your ba - by. _____ (Your ba - by.) Ech-oes (ech-oes)

of your name in - side my mind. Ha - lo, hid - ing my ob - ses - sion. I

once was poi - son i - vy, but now I'm your dai - sy. _____

And, ba - by, for ___ you, ___

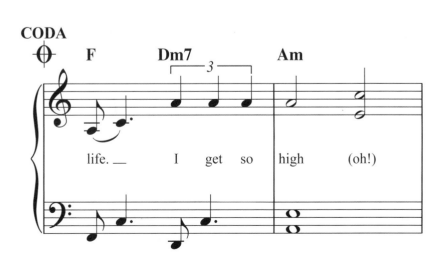

life. ___ I get so high (oh!)

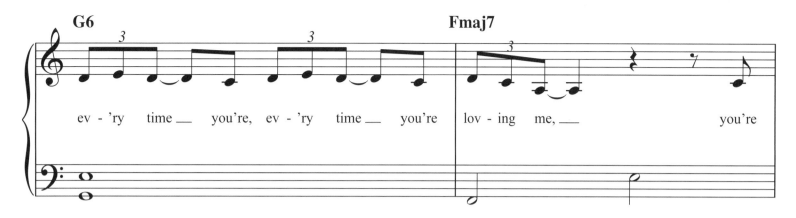

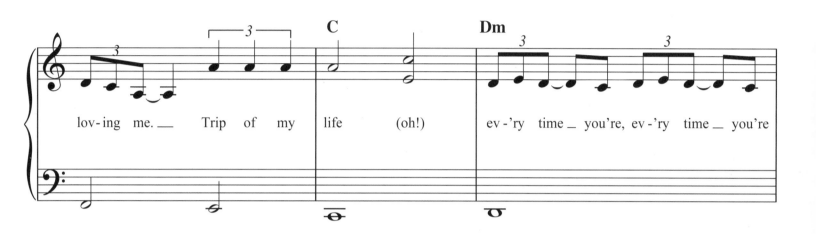

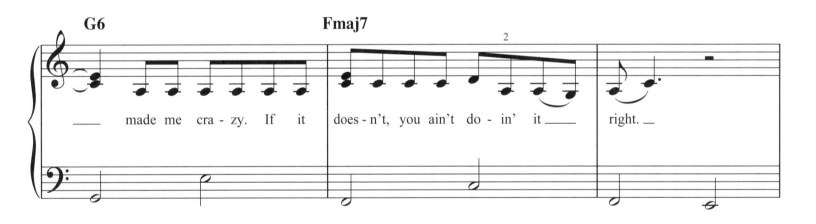

31

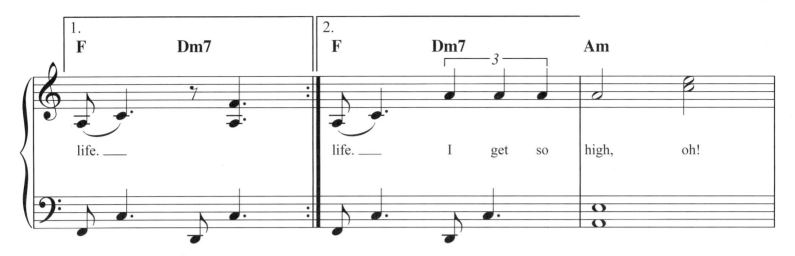

DELICATE

Words and Music by TAYLOR SWIFT,
MAX MARTIN and SHELLBACK

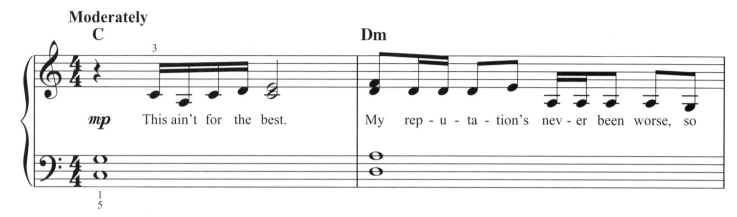

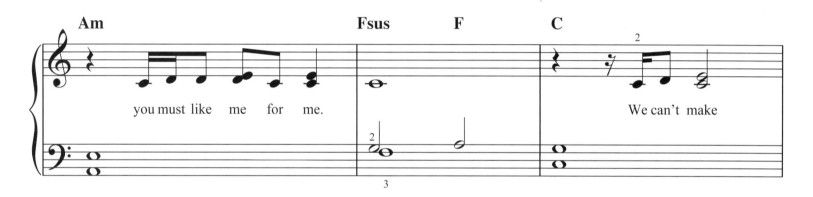

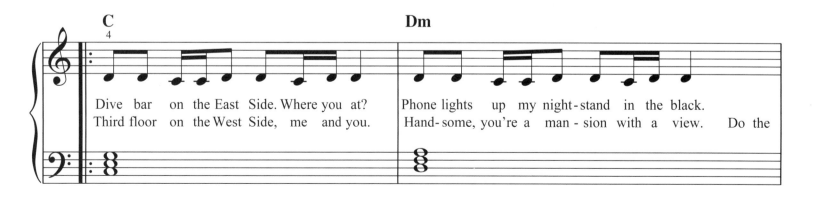

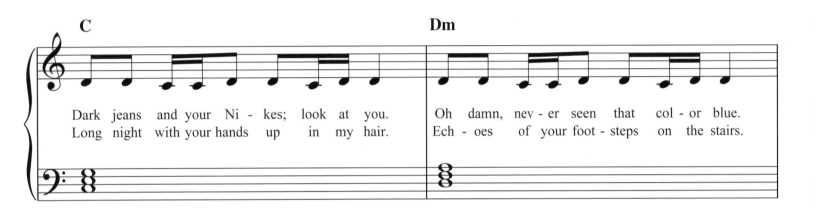

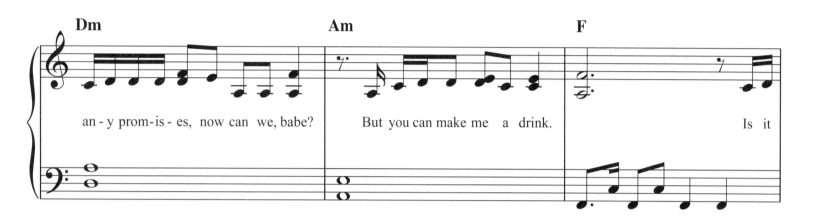

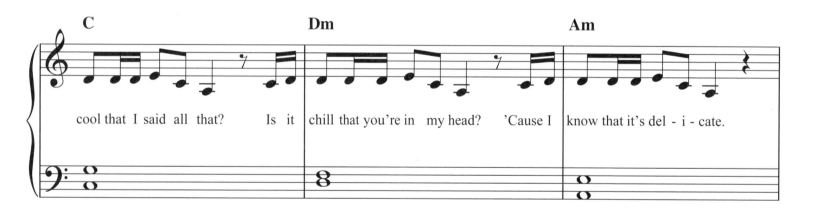

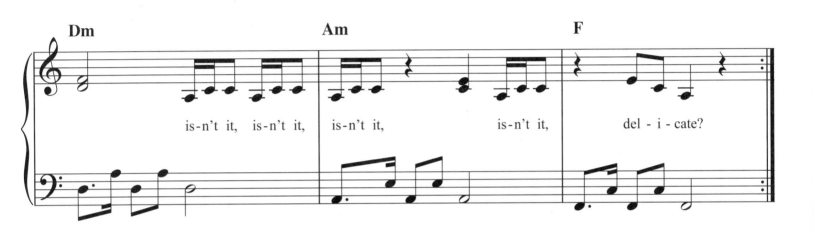

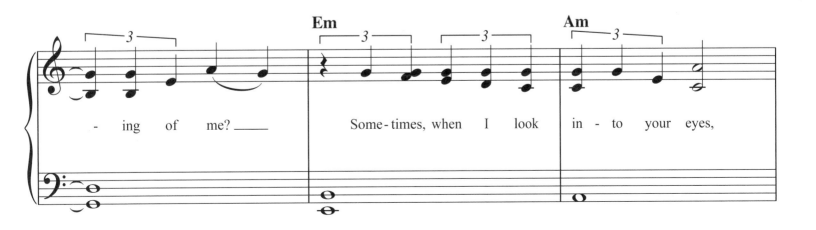

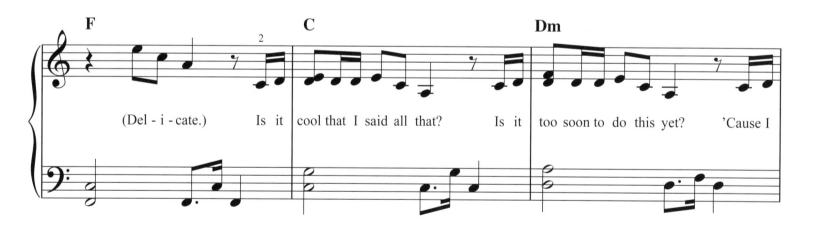

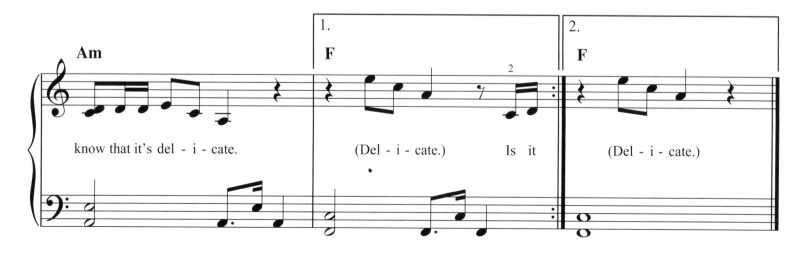

LOOK WHAT YOU MADE ME DO

Words and Music by TAYLOR SWIFT,
JACK ANTONOFF, RICHARD FAIRBRASS,
FRED FAIRBRASS and ROB MANZOLI

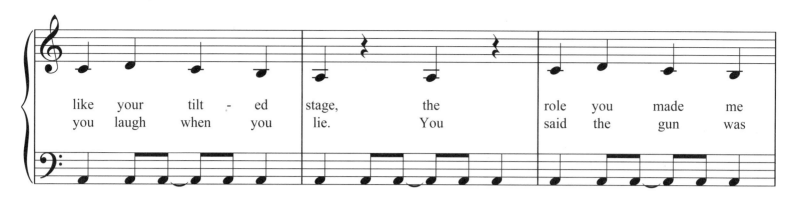

like your tilt - ed stage, the role you made me
you laugh when you lie. You said the gun was

1.

2.

play of the fool. No, I don't like you.
mine. Is-n't cool. No, I don't like you.

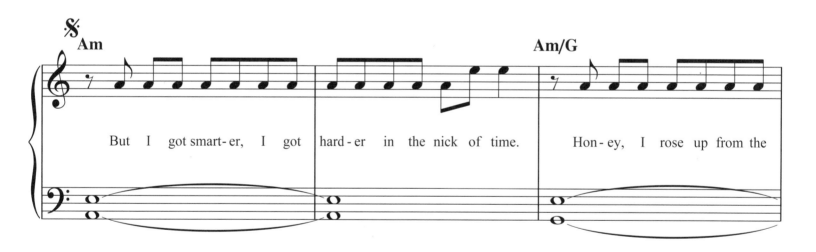

Am   **Am/G**

But I got smart-er, I got hard-er in the nick of time. Hon-ey, I rose up from the

F

dead. I do it all the time. I've got a list of names and yours is in red, un-der-lined,

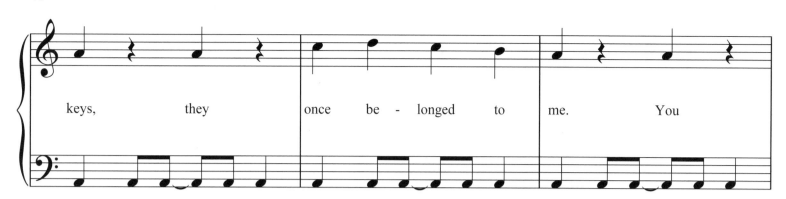

keys, they once be - longed to me. You

asked me for a place to sleep, locked me out and threw a feast.

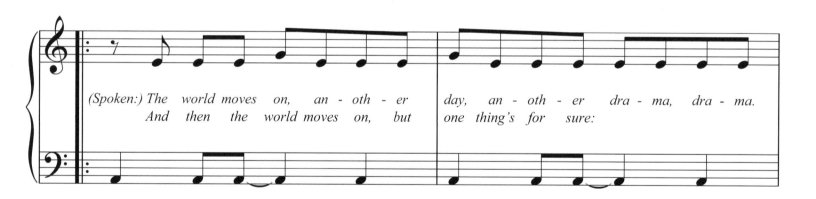

(Spoken:) The world moves on, an - oth - er day, an - oth - er dra - ma, dra - ma.
And then the world moves on, but one thing's for sure:

D.S. al Coda

1. 2.

But not for me, not for me, all I think a - bout is kar - ma.
May - be I got mine, but you'll all get yours.

CODA

me do, look what you just made me... I don't trust no - bod - y and no -

bod - y trusts me.   I'll be the ac - tress   star - ring in your bad dreams.

star - ring in your bad dreams.   I don't trust no - bod - y and no - bod - y trusts me.

I'll be the ac - tress   star - ring in your bad dreams.   star - ring in your bad dreams.

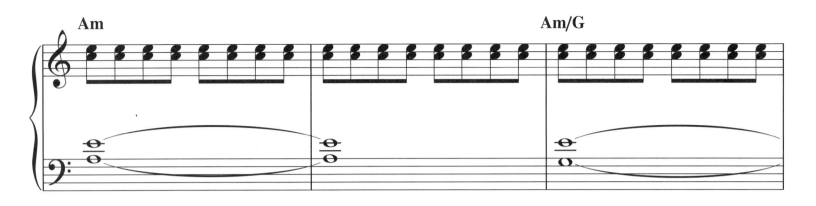

(Spoken:) "I'm sorry, the old Taylor   can't come to the phone right now.   Why?

Oh,   'cause she's dead!"   (Sung:) Ooh,   look what you made me

do,   look what you made me   do.   Look what you just made   me do, look what you just made me...

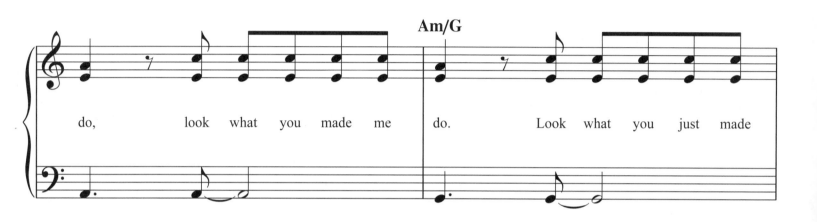

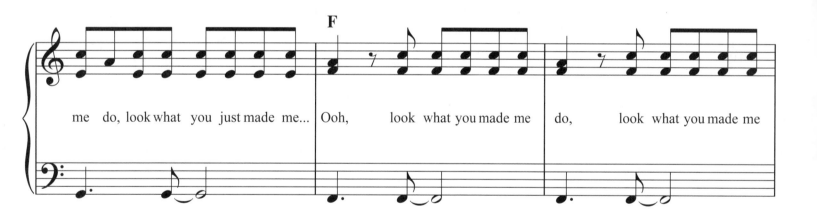

SO IT GOES . . .

Words and Music by TAYLOR SWIFT,
MAX MARTIN, SHELLBACK
and OSCAR GORRES

Slowly

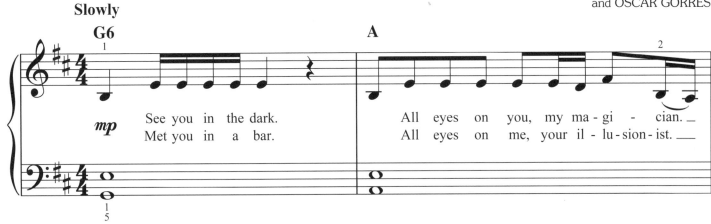

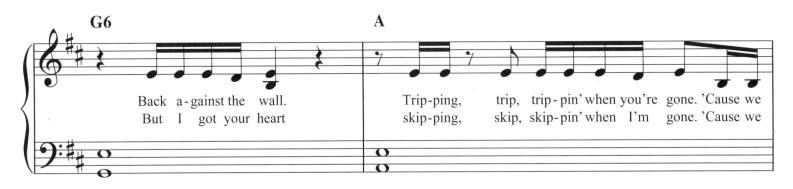

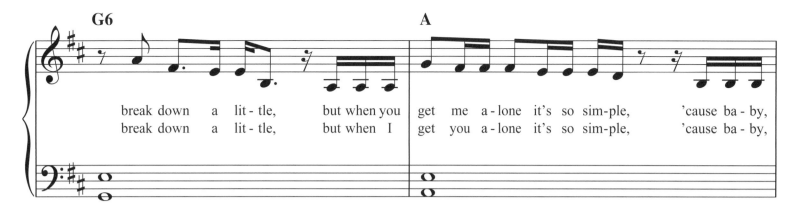

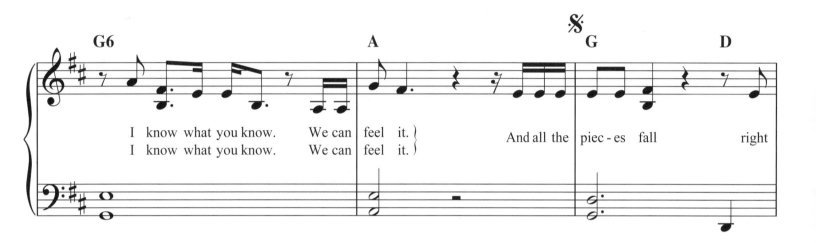

yours to ___ lose. You know I'm not a bad girl, but I do bad

things with _ you. So it goes. ___ Come here, dressed in black now. So, so, so it goes. ___

Scratch-es down your back now. So, so, so it goes. ___

You did a num-ber on me, but hon-est-ly, ba-by, who's count-ing?

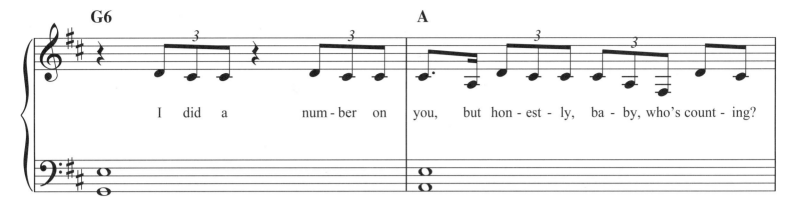

I did a num-ber on you, but hon-est-ly, ba-by, who's count-ing?

You did a num-ber on me, but hon-est-ly, ba-by, who's count-ing? Who's count-ing?

One, two, three. And all the

Come here, dressed in black now.

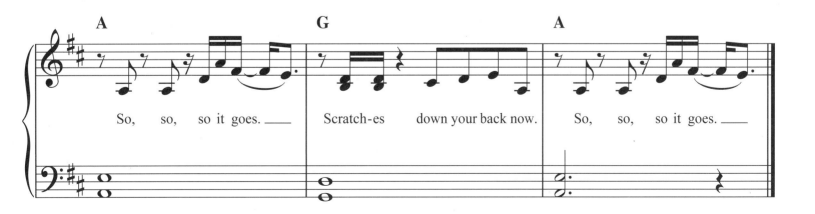

So, so, so it goes. Scratch-es down your back now. So, so, so it goes.

GORGEOUS

Words and Music by TAYLOR SWIFT,
MAX MARTIN and SHELLBACK

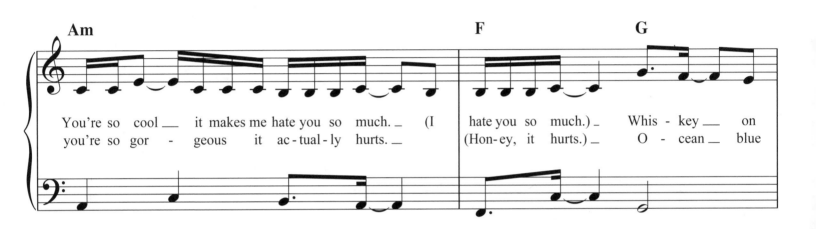

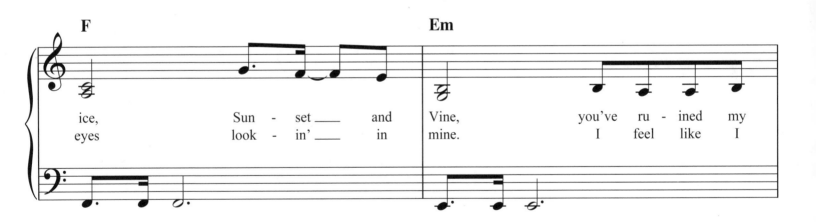

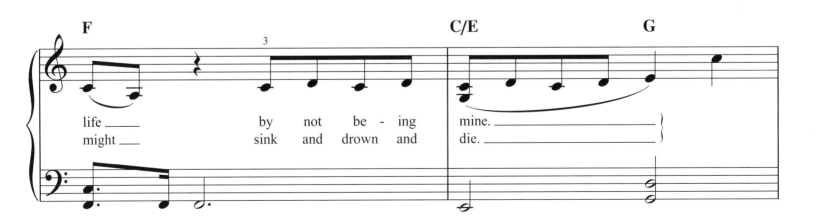

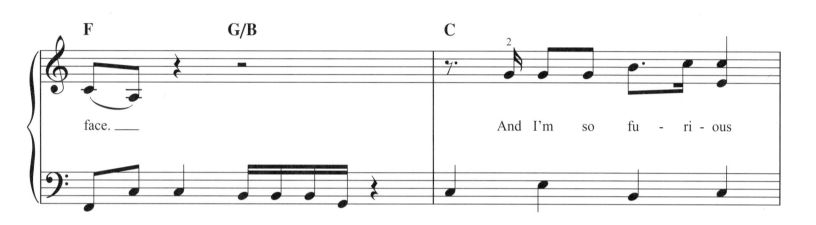

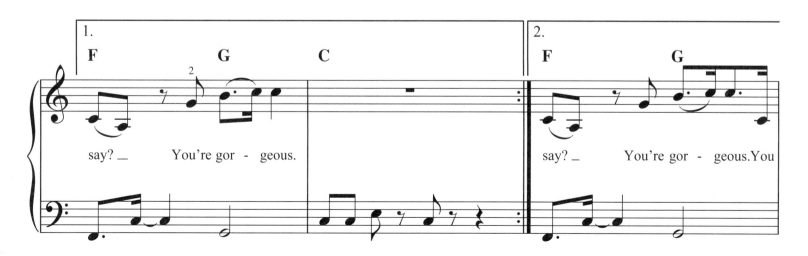

51

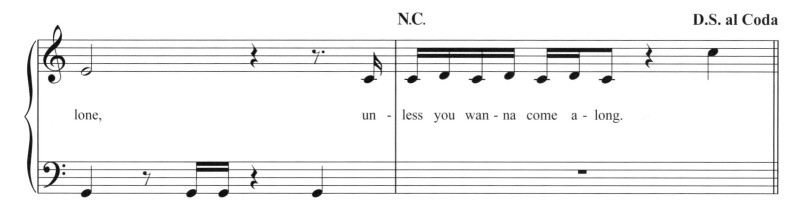

GETAWAY CAR

Words and Music by TAYLOR SWIFT
and JACK ANTONOFF

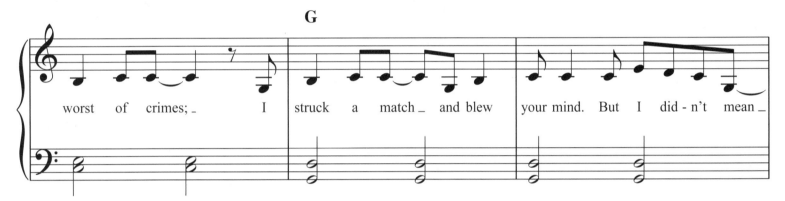

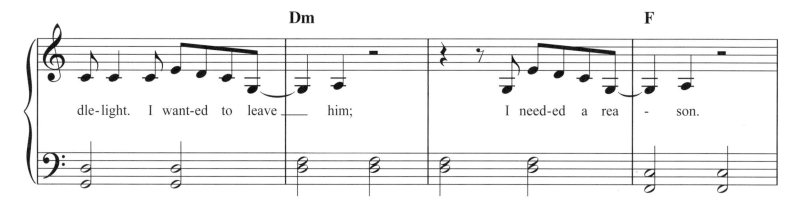

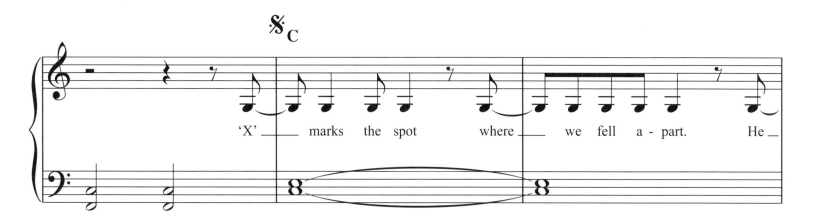

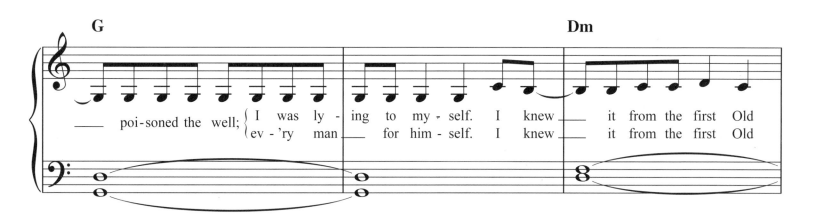

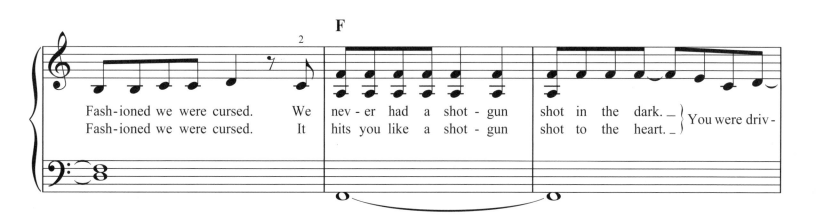

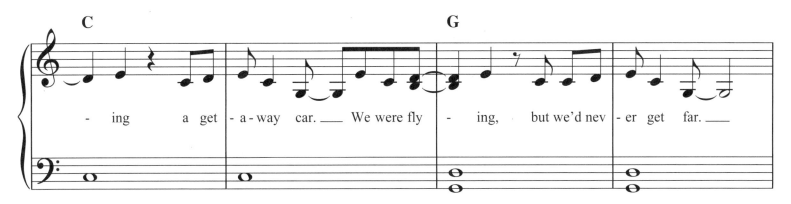

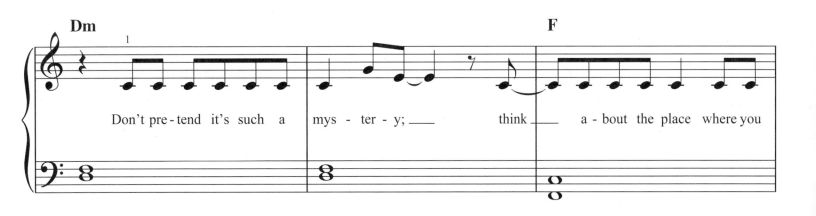

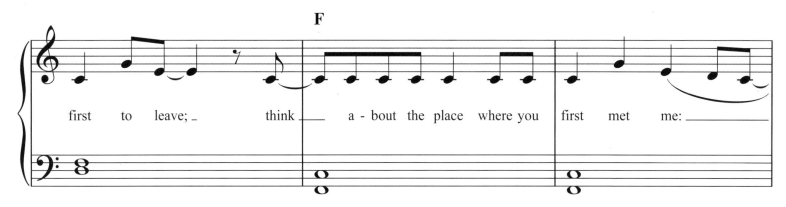

first to leave; _ think _ a - bout the place where you first met me: _____

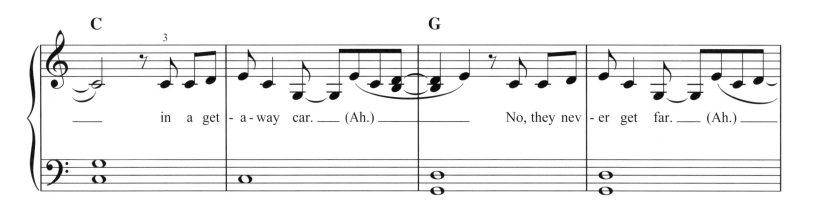

_____ in a get - a - way car. _ (Ah.) _____ No, they nev - er get far. _ (Ah.) _____

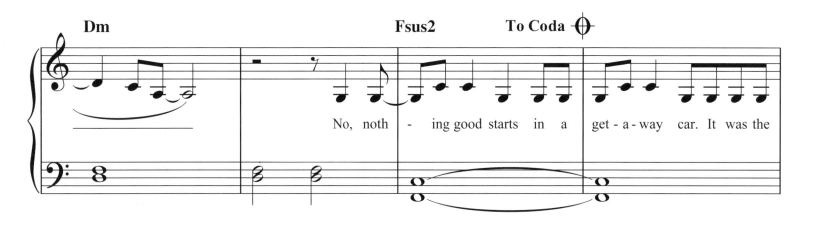

_____ No, noth - ing good starts in a get - a - way car. It was the

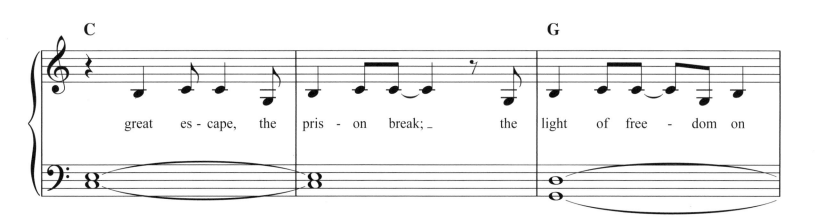

great es - cape, the pris - on break; _ the light of free - dom on

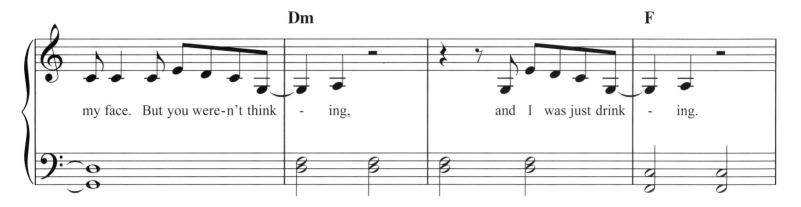

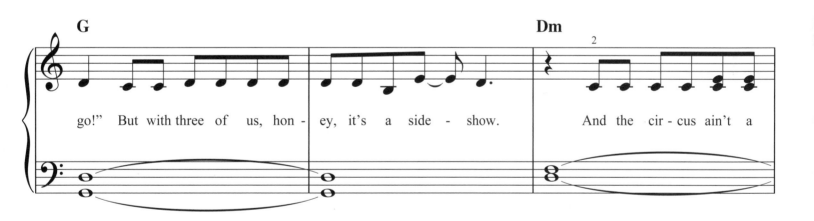

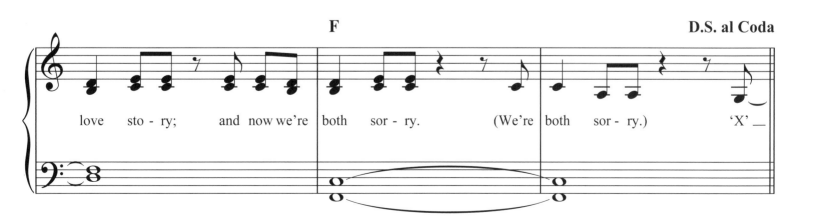

58

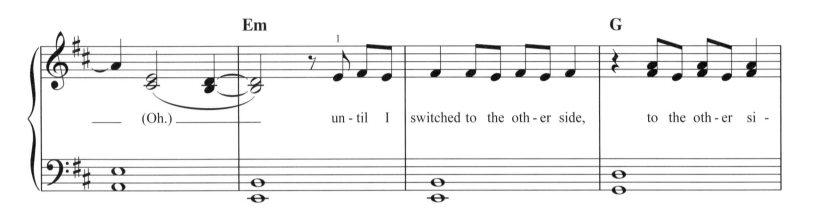

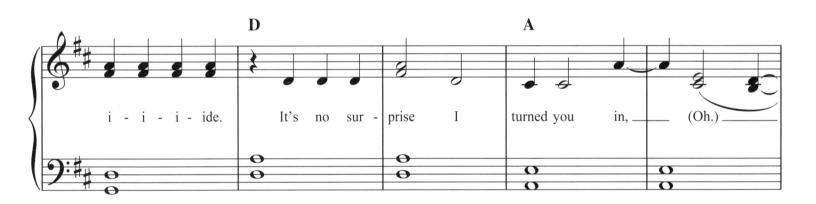

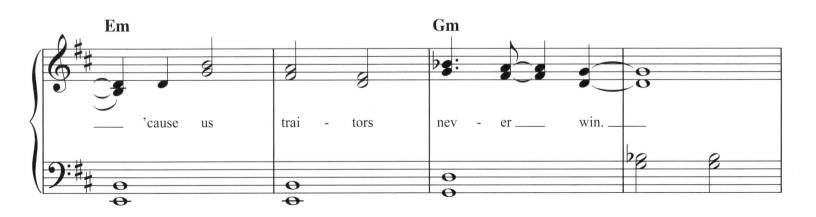

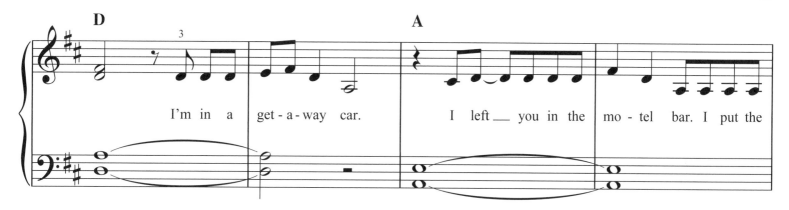

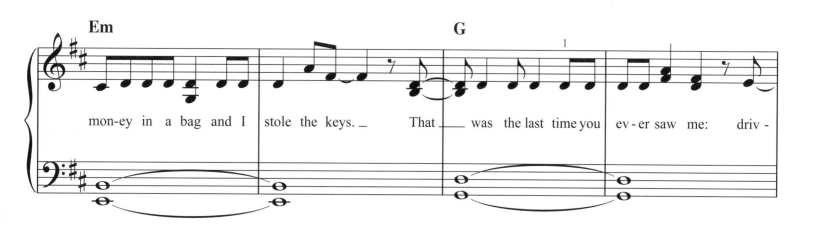

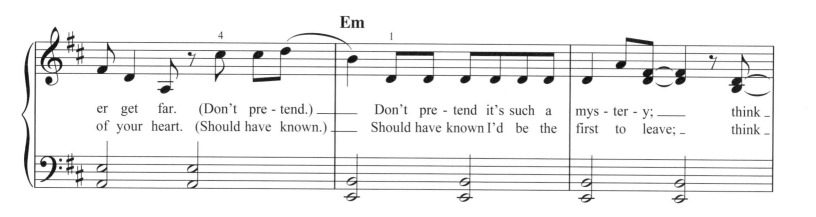

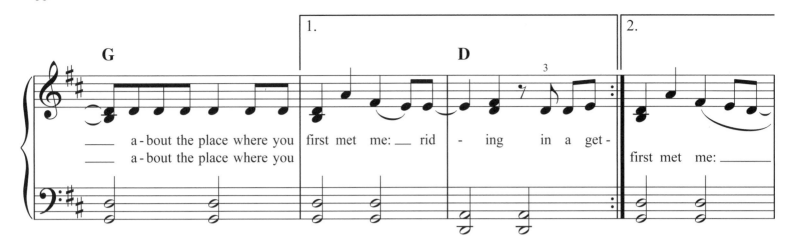

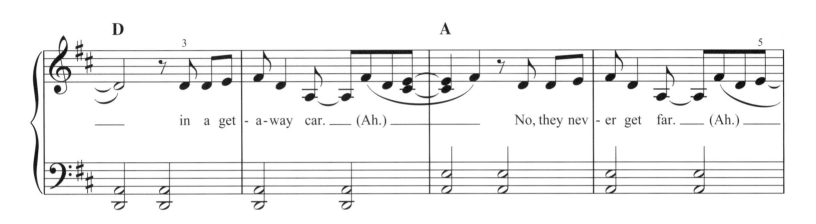

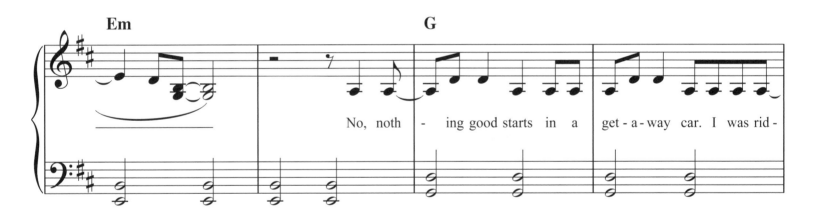

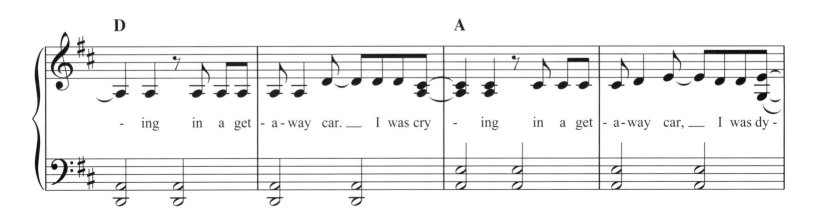

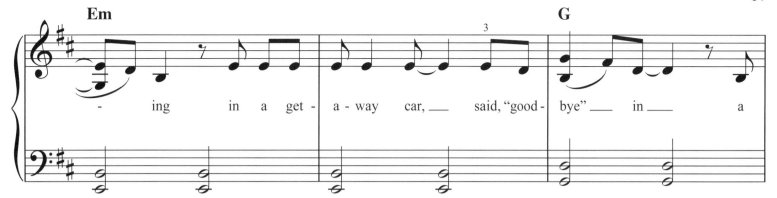

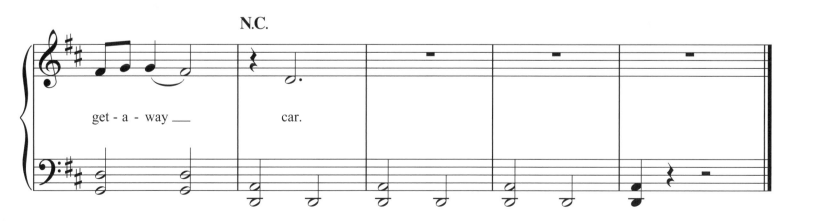

KING OF MY HEART

Words and Music by TAYLOR SWIFT,
MAX MARTIN and SHELLBACK

Moderately fast

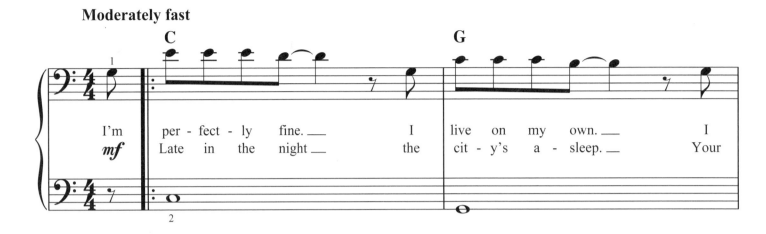

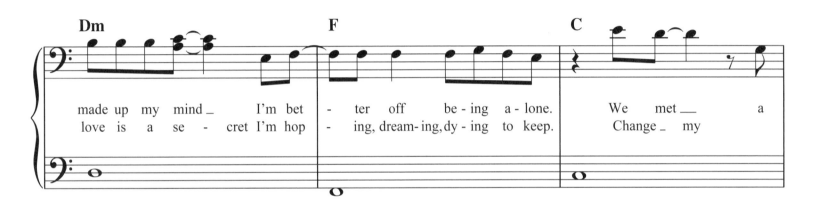

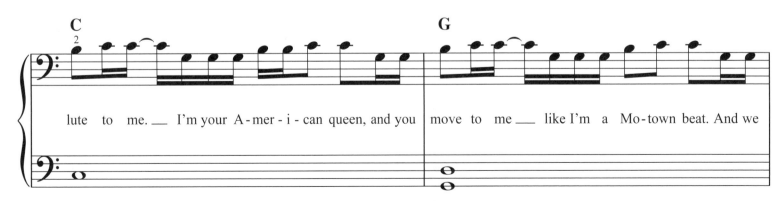

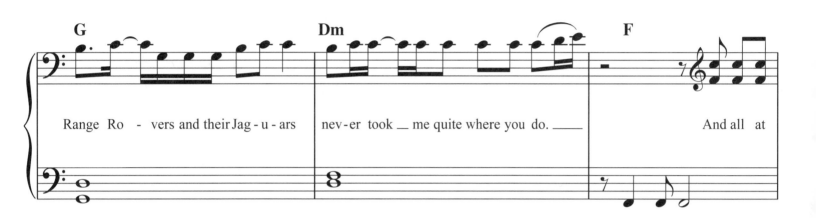

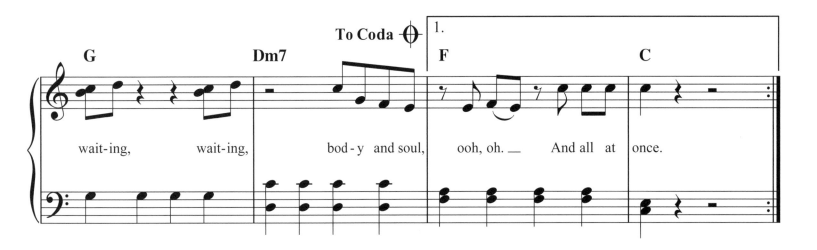

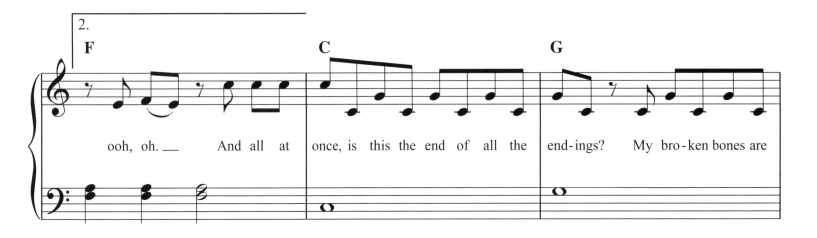

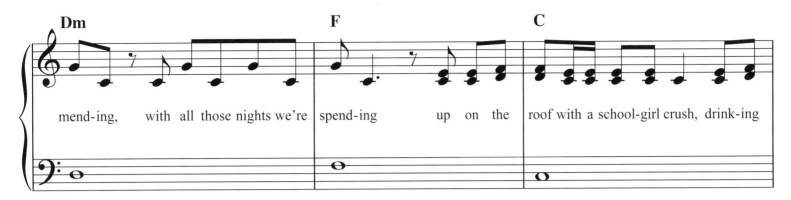

mend-ing, with all those nights we're spend-ing up on the roof with a school-girl crush, drink-ing

beer out of plas-tic cups. Say you fan-cy me, not fan-cy stuff. Ba-by, all at once this is e-nough. (And all at

once you are the one I have been wait-ing for, king of my heart, bod-y and soul,

ooh, oh, oh.) And all at

ooh, oh. ___ And all at once.

DANCING WITH OUR HANDS TIED

Words and Music by TAYLOR SWIFT,
MAX MARTIN, SHELLBACK
and OSCAR HOLTER

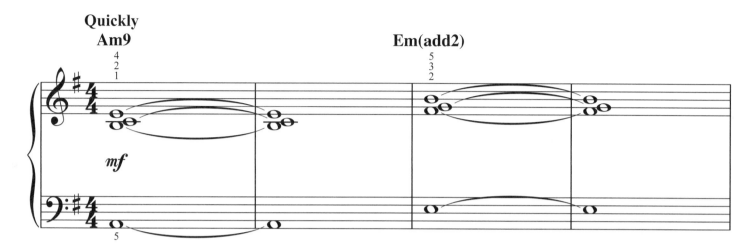

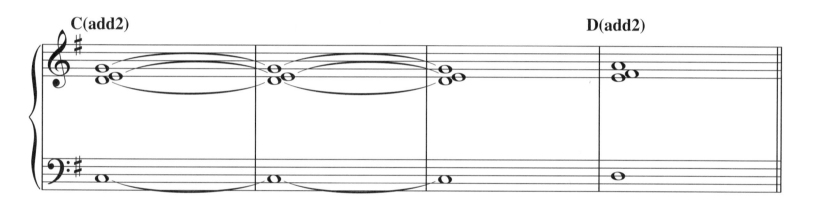

I, ___ I loved you in se - cret.
loved you in spite of

First sight, yeah, we
deep fears that the

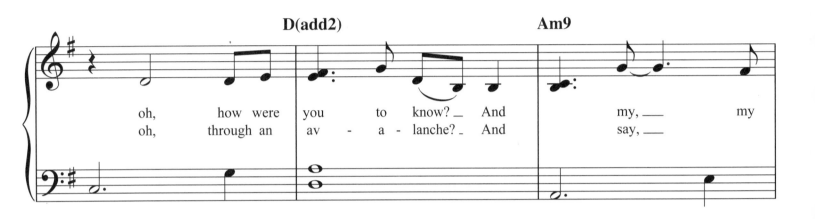

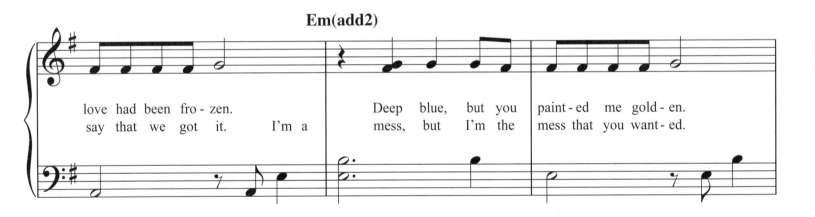

could have spent for-ev-er with your | hands in my pock-ets.
you had turned my bed in-to a | sa-cred o-a-sis.
could have spent for-ev-er with your | hands in my pock-ets.

Pic-ture of your face in an in-
Peo-ple start-ed talk-ing, put-ting
Pic-ture of your face in an in-

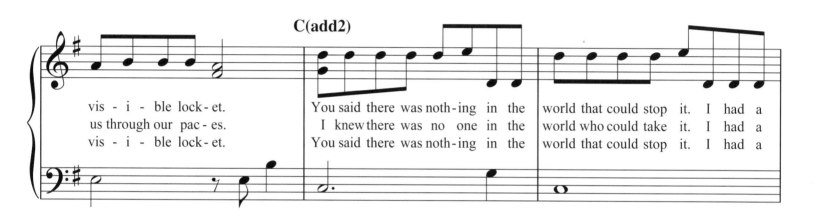

vis - i - ble lock-et.
us through our pac-es.
vis - i - ble lock-et.

You said there was noth-ing in the
I knew there was no one in the
You said there was noth-ing in the

world that could stop it. I had a
world who could take it. I had a
world that could stop it. I had a

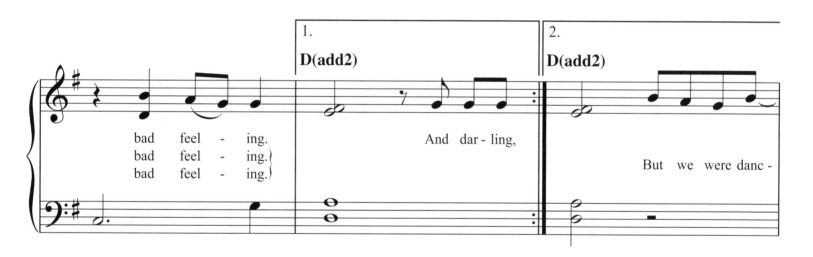

bad feel - ing.
bad feel - ing.
bad feel - ing.

And dar - ling,

But we were danc -

- ing,

danc - ing with our

hands tied, hands _

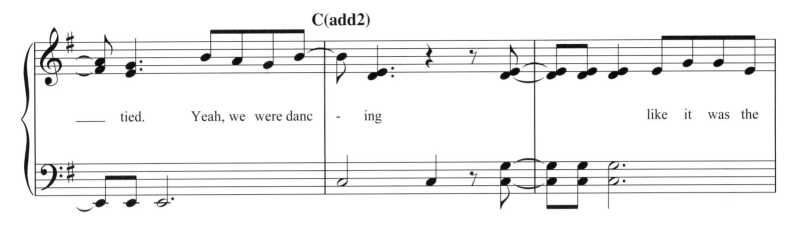

C(add2)

tied.   Yeah, we were danc - ing   like it was the

D   Am9

first   time,   first ____ time.   Yeah, we were danc - ing,

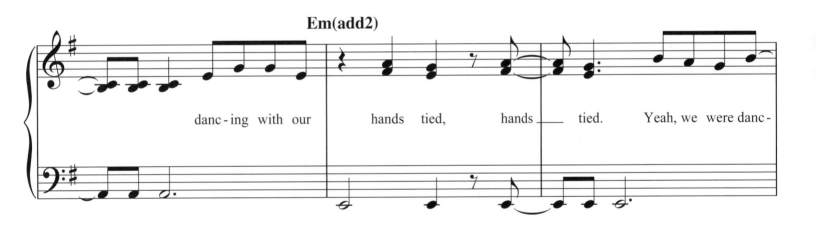

Em(add2)

danc - ing with our   hands tied,   hands ____ tied.   Yeah, we were danc-

C(add2)   To Coda

- ing   and I had a   bad   feel - ing.____

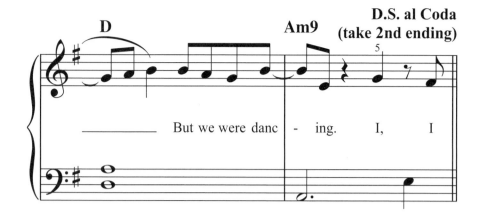

But we were danc - ing. I, I

But we were danc-

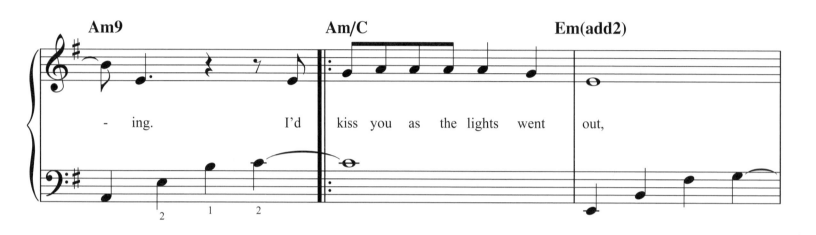

- ing.   I'd   kiss you   as   the lights went   out,

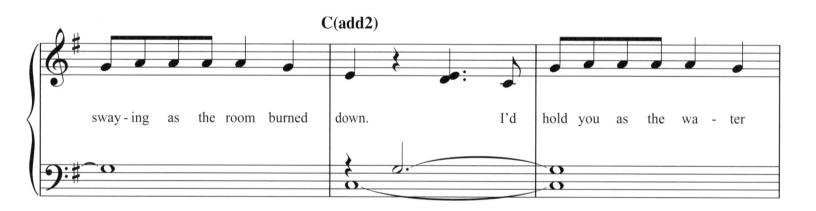

sway - ing as the room burned   down.   I'd   hold you as the wa - ter

rush - es   in,   if   I could dance with   you   a - gain.   I'd

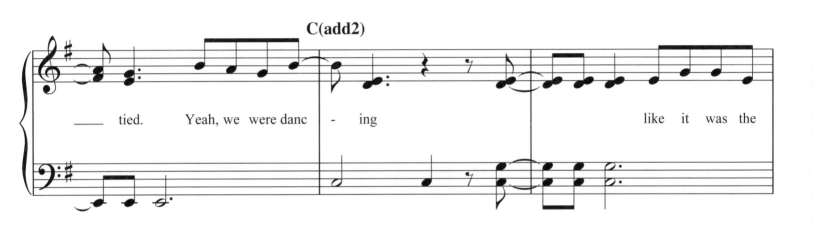

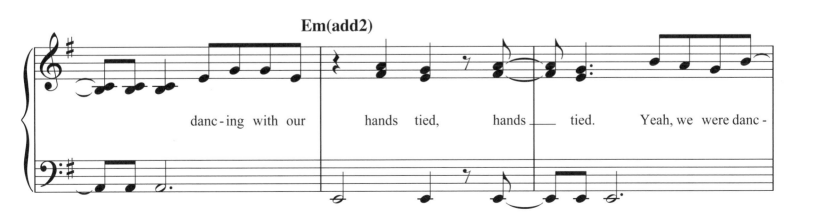

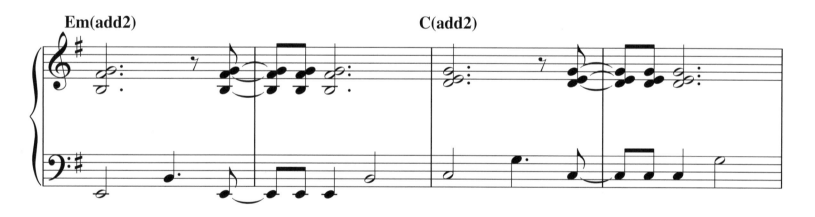

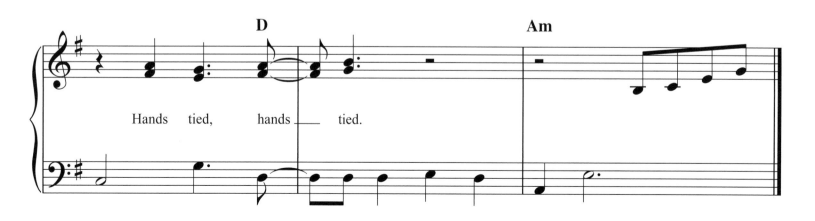

NEW YEAR'S DAY

Words and Music by TAYLOR SWIFT
and JACK ANTONOFF

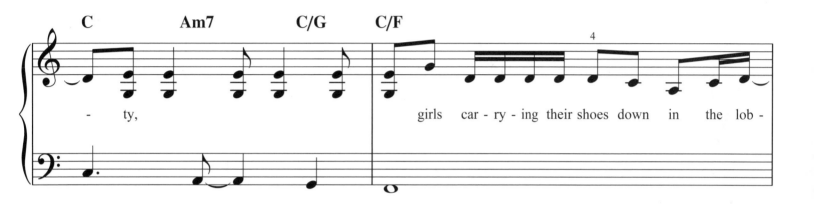

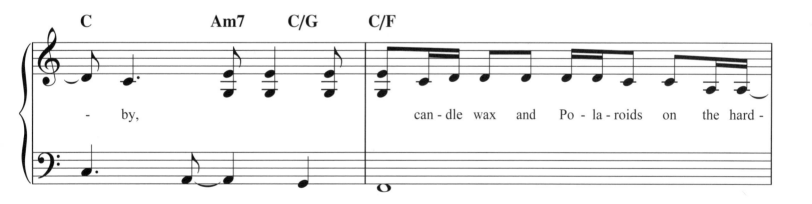

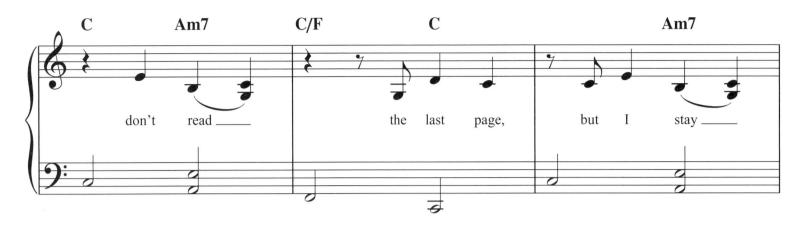

don't read ___ the last page, but I stay ___

when you're lost, ___ and I'm scared, ___ and you're turn - ing a - way. I want ___

your mid - nights, but I'll be clean-ing up bot - tles with you ___ on

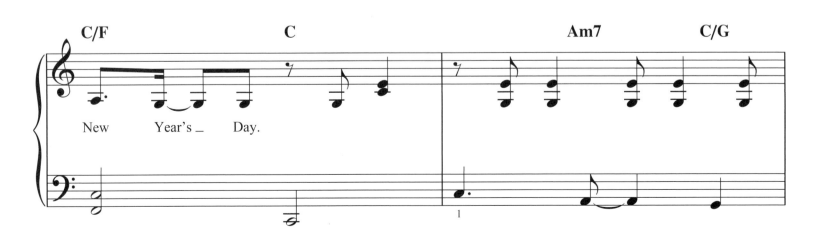

New Year's ___ Day.

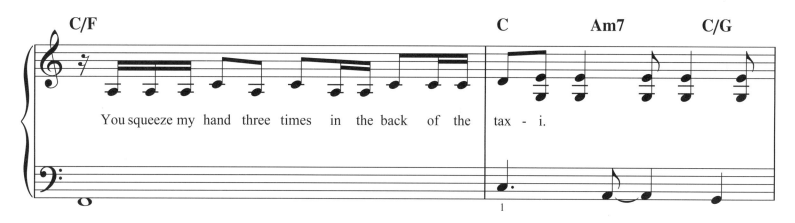

You squeeze my hand three times in the back of the tax - i.

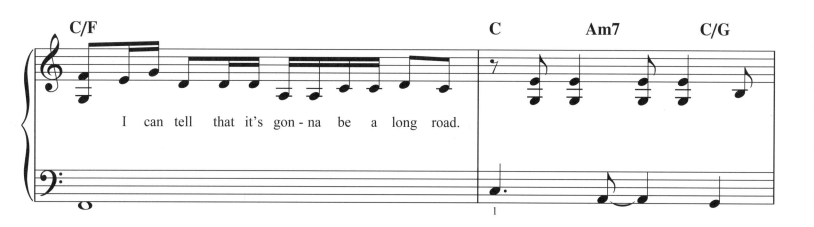

I can tell that it's gon - na be a long road.

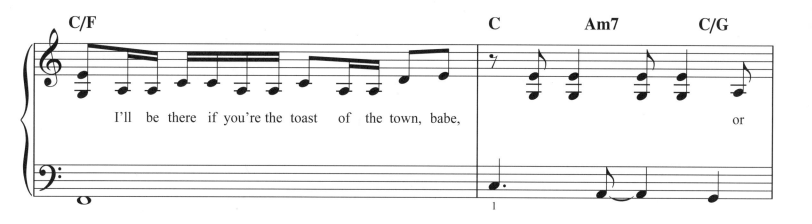

I'll be there if you're the toast of the town, babe, or

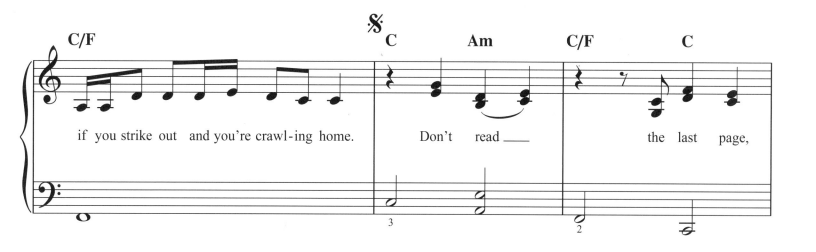

if you strike out and you're crawl-ing home. Don't read ___ the last page,

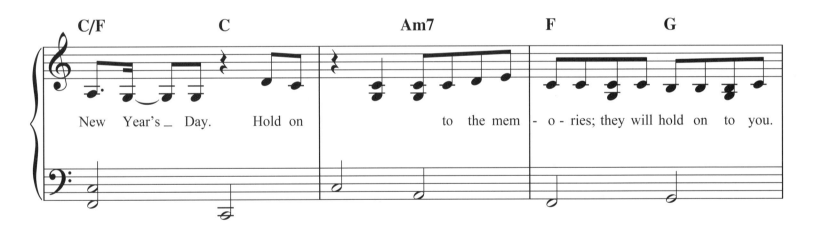

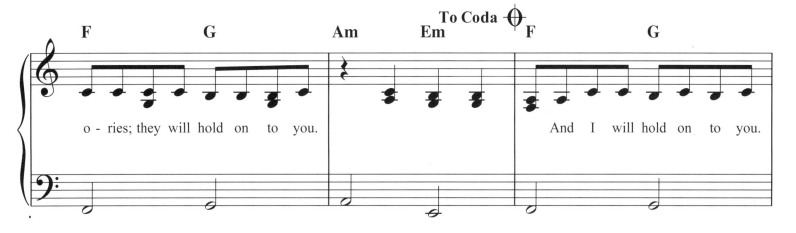

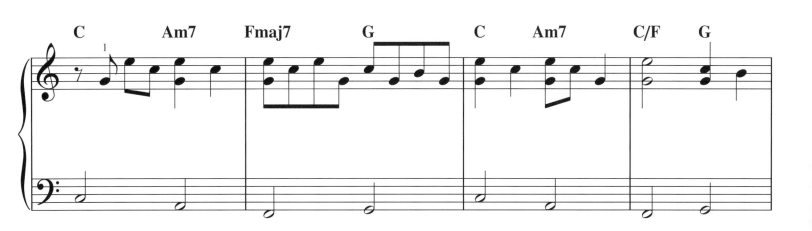

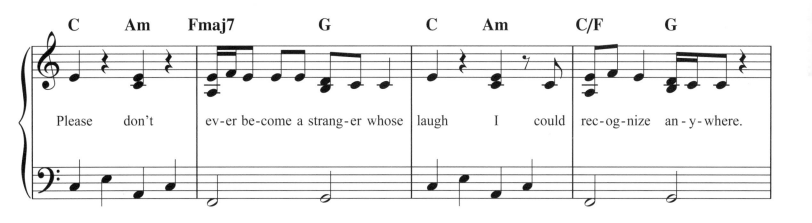

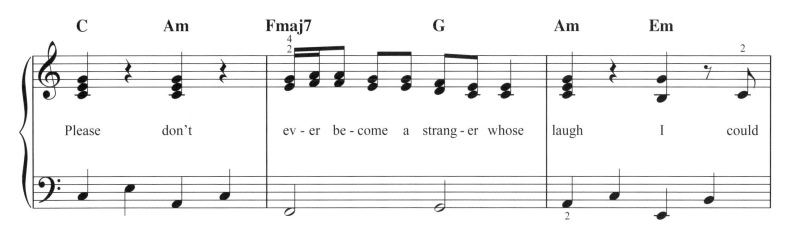

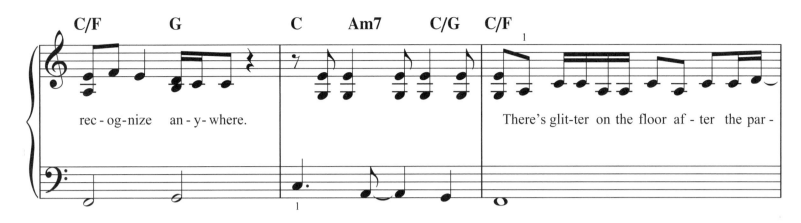

rec - og-nize   an - y-where.   There's glit-ter on the floor af - ter the par-

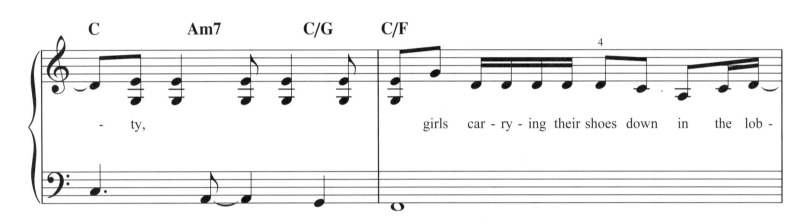

- ty,   girls car - ry - ing their shoes down in the lob-

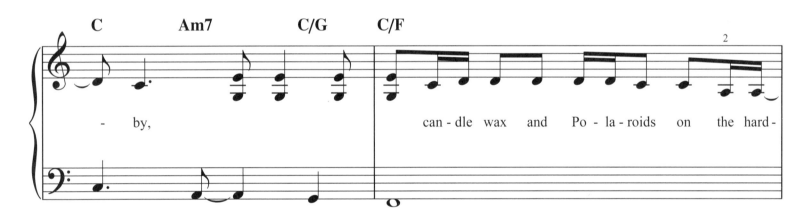

- by,   can - dle wax and Po - la - roids on the hard-

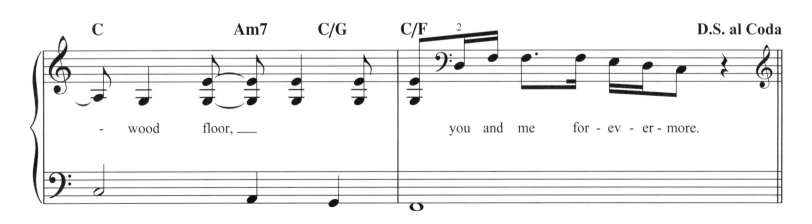

- wood   floor, ___   you and me   for - ev - er - more.

D.S. al Coda

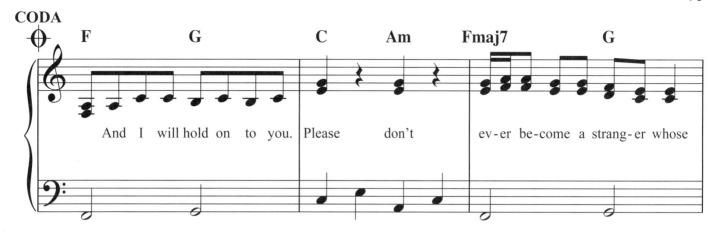

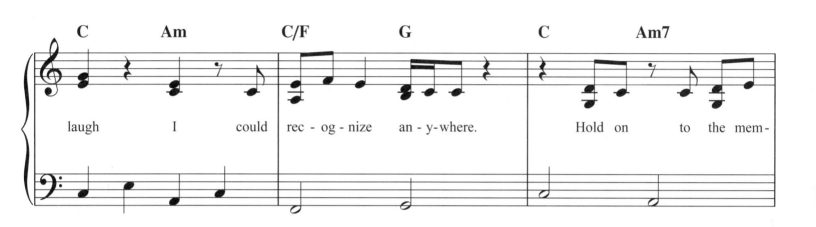

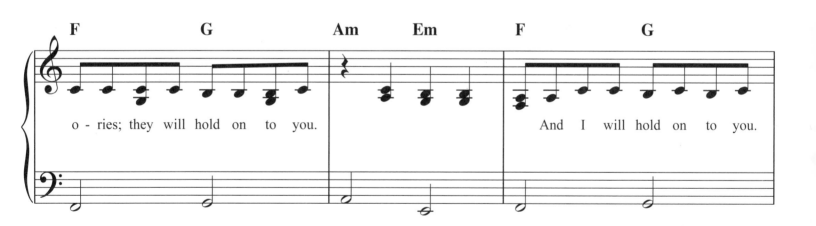

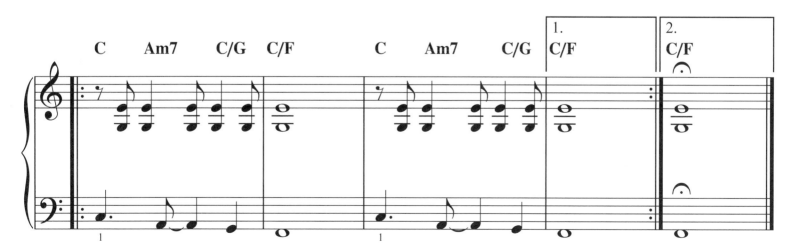

DRESS

Words and Music by TAYLOR SWIFT
and JACK ANTONOFF

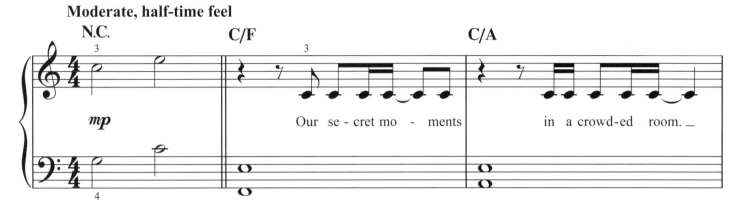

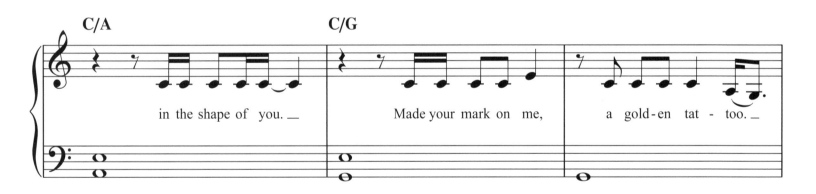

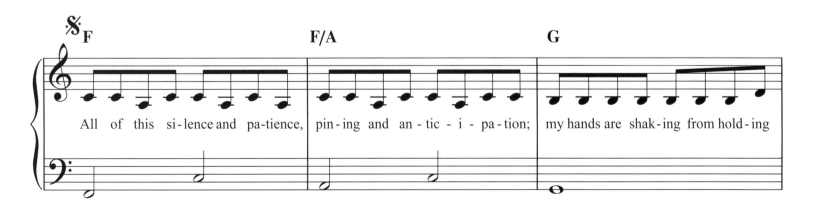

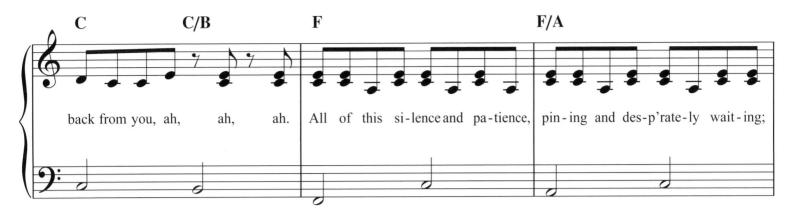

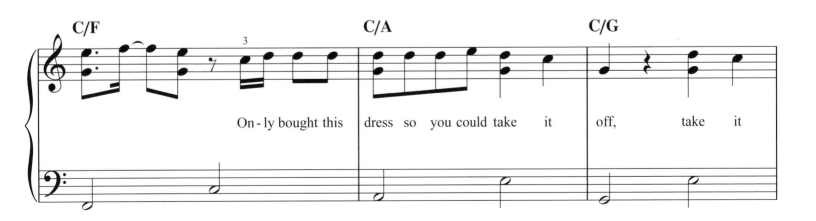

off, ah, ah, ahh. Carve your name in - to my bed - post,

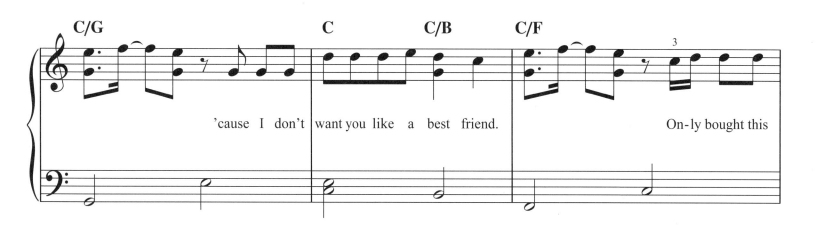

'cause I don't want you like a best friend. On-ly bought this

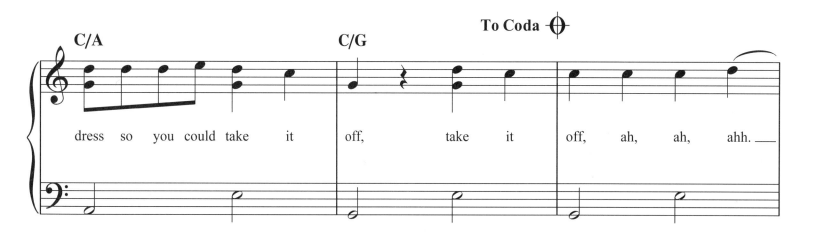

dress so you could take it off, take it off, ah, ah, ahh.

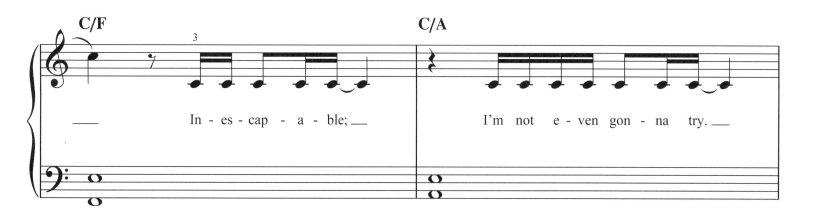

In - es - cap - a - ble; I'm not e - ven gon - na try.

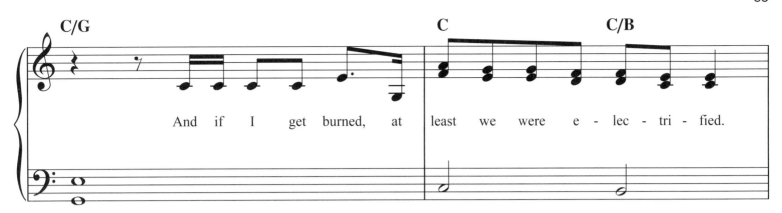

And if I get burned, at least we were e - lec - tri - fied.

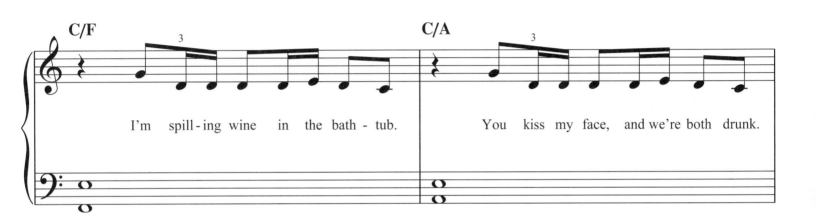

I'm spill-ing wine in the bath - tub.

You kiss my face, and we're both drunk.

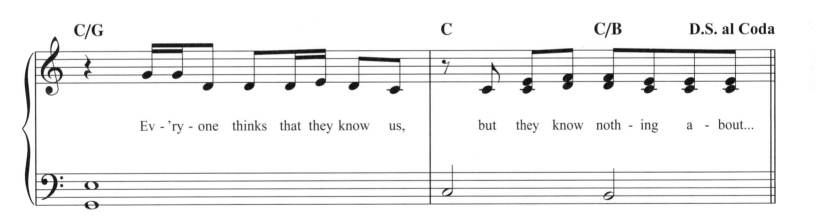

Ev -'ry - one thinks that they know us,

but they know noth - ing a - bout...

D.S. al Coda

CODA

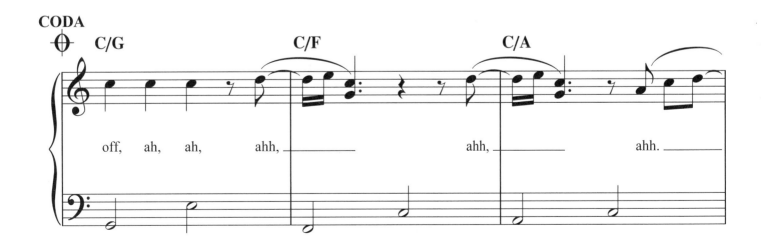

off, ah, ah, ahh,

ahh,

ahh.

you saw the truth in me. And I woke up just ___ in time; now I

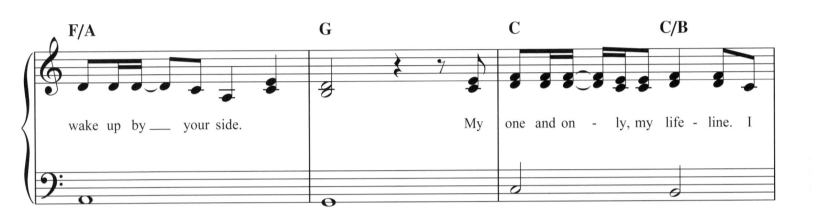

wake up by ___ your side. My one and on - ly, my life - line. I

woke up just ___ in time; now I wake up by ___ your side. My

hands shake, ___ I can't ex - plain ___ this ah, ah, ah, ahh. ___ Say my

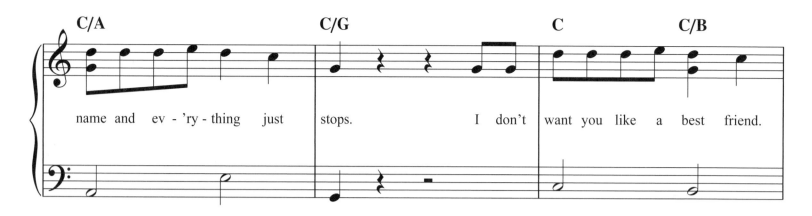

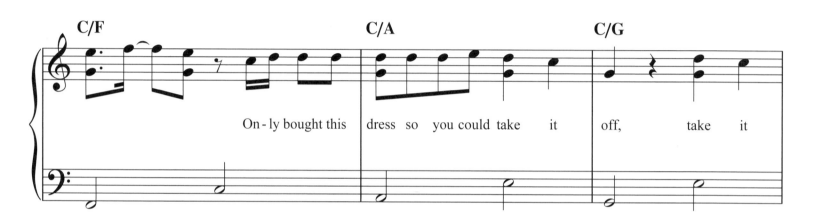

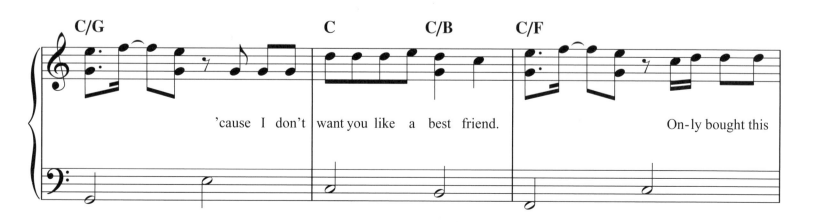

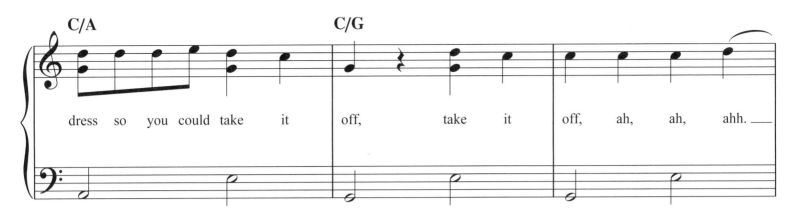

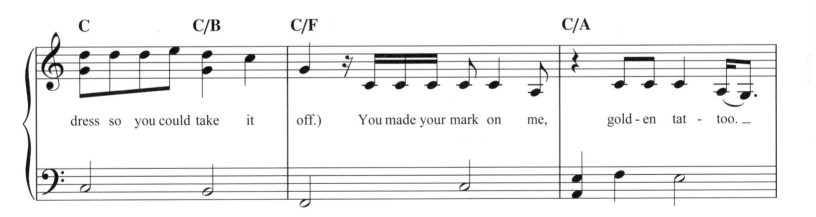

THIS IS WHY WE CAN'T HAVE NICE THINGS

Words and Music by TAYLOR SWIFT
and JACK ANTONOFF

Moderately, in 2

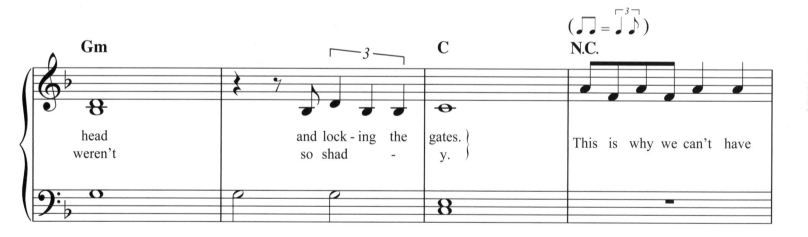

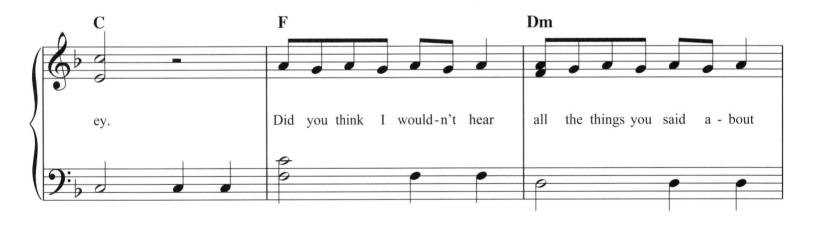

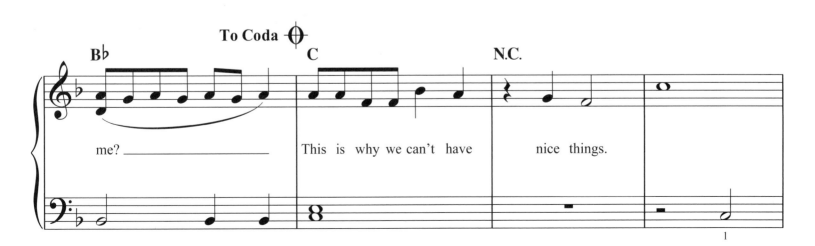

It was so nice be - ing friends a - gain. There I was,

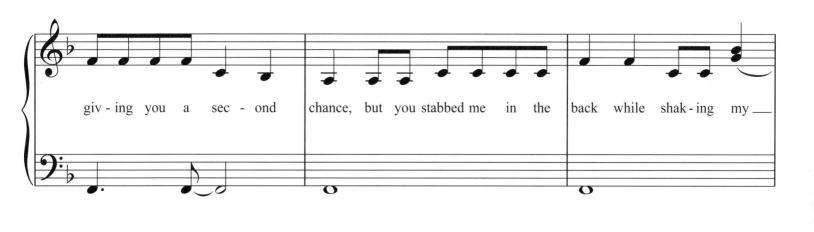

giv - ing you a sec - ond chance, but you stabbed me in the back while shak - ing my ___

___ hand. ___ And there-in lies the is - sue: friends don't try to

trick you, get you on the phone and mind - twist you. And so I took an

92

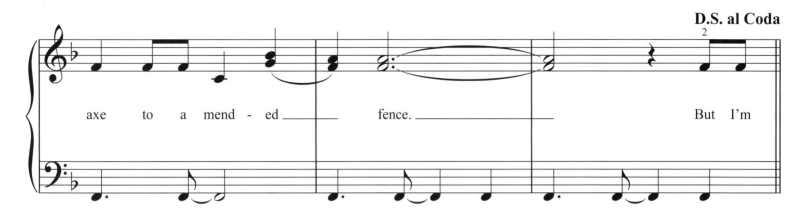

axe to a mend - ed _____ fence. _____   But I'm

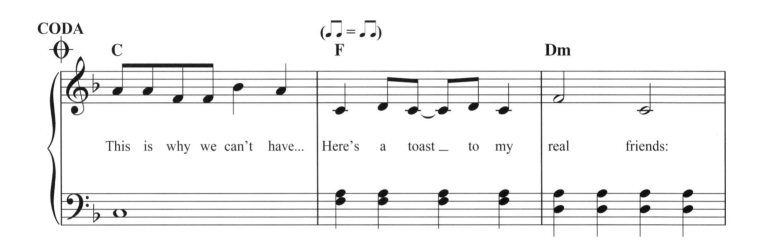

This is why we can't have... Here's a toast _ to my   real   friends:

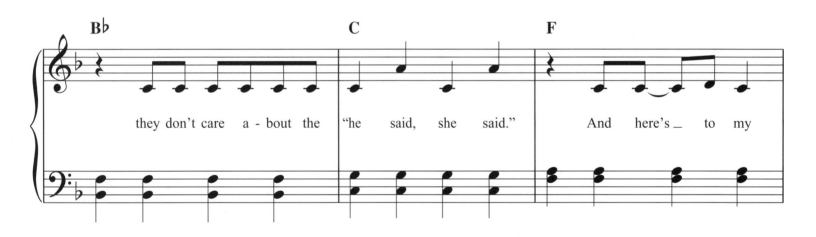

they don't care a - bout the   "he   said,   she   said."   And here's _ to my

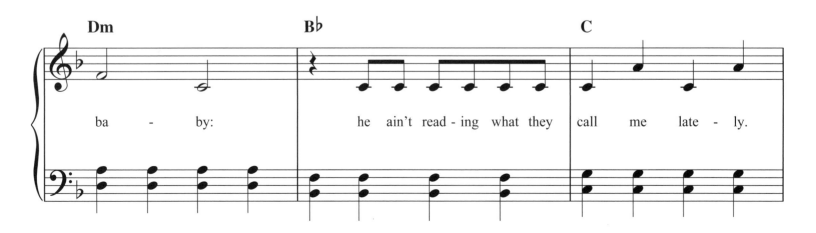

ba - by: he ain't read - ing what they   call   me late - ly.

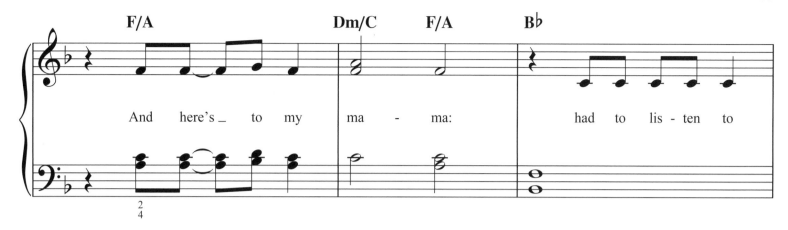

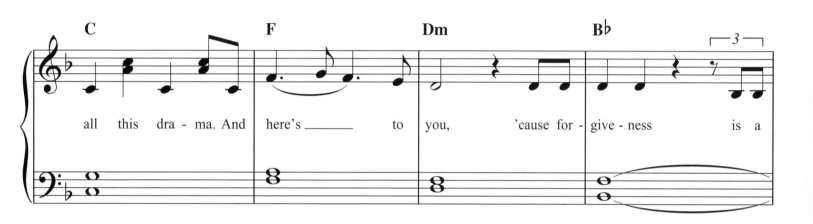

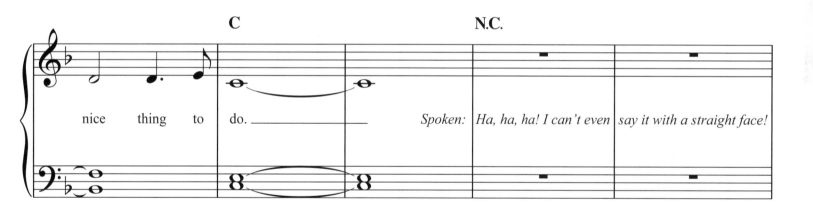

95

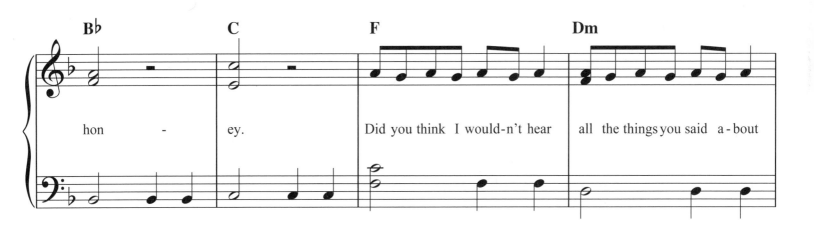

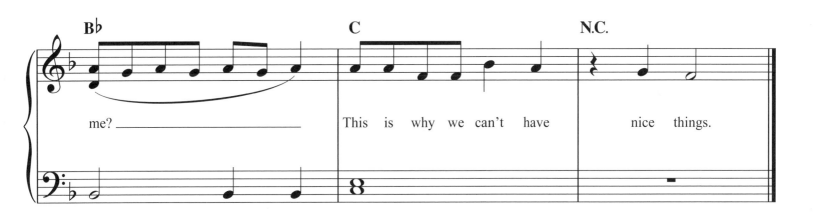

CALL IT WHAT YOU WANT

Words and Music by TAYLOR SWIFT
and JACK ANTONOFF

better than I ev-er was.___ 'Cause my ba-by's

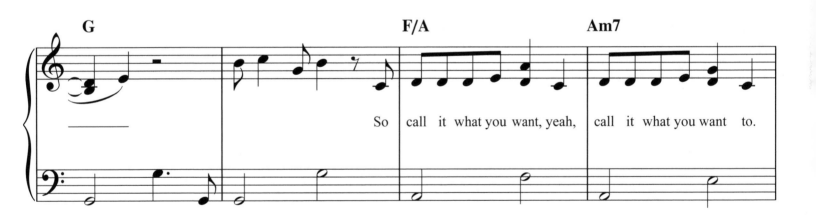

fit like a day-dream, walk-in' with his head down. I'm the one he's walk-in' to.___

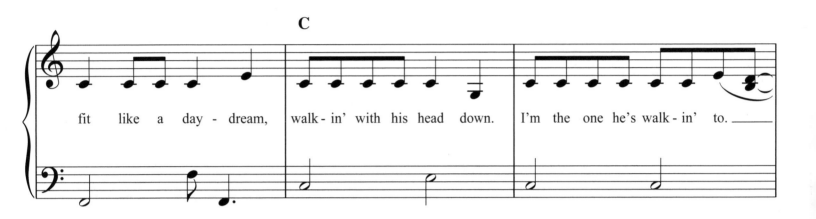

___ So call it what you want, yeah, call it what you want to.

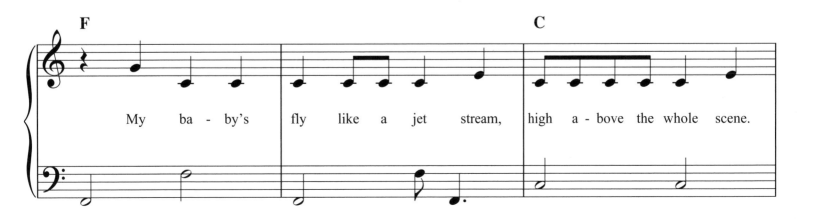

My ba-by's fly like a jet stream, high a-bove the whole scene.

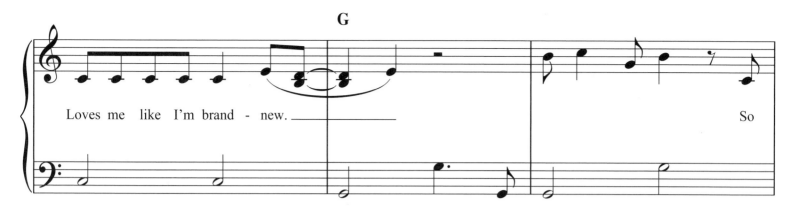

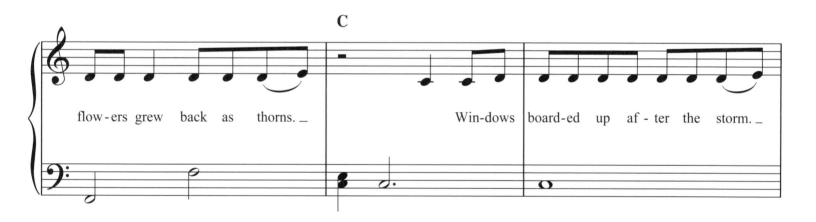

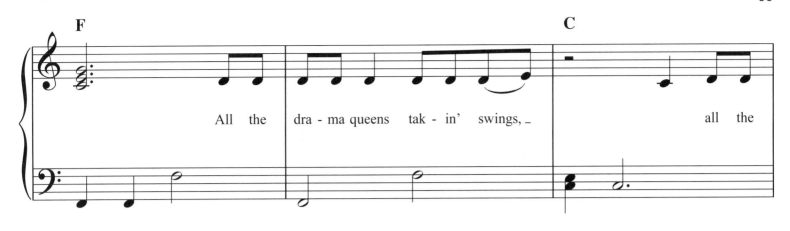

F　　　　　　　　　　　　　　　　　　　**C**

All the dra - ma queens tak - in' swings, _ all the

G

jok - ers dress - in' up as kings. _ They fade to noth - in' when I look at him. _

F/A　　　　**Am7**　　　　**F**

And I know I make the same mis-takes ev -'ry time.

C　　　　　　　　　　　　　　　　　　　**G**

Bridg - es burn, I nev - er learn. At least I did one thing right, _

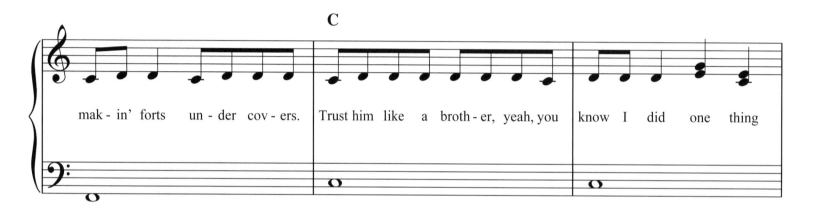

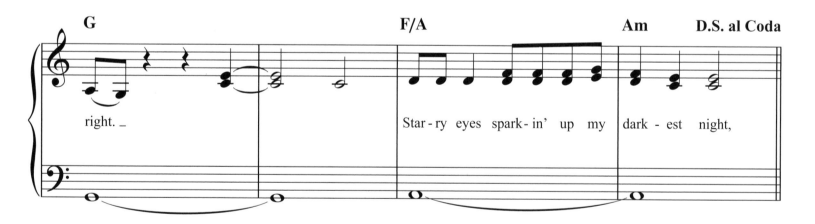

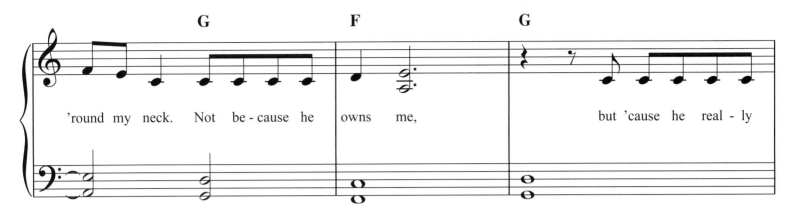

'round my neck. Not be-cause he owns me, but 'cause he real-ly

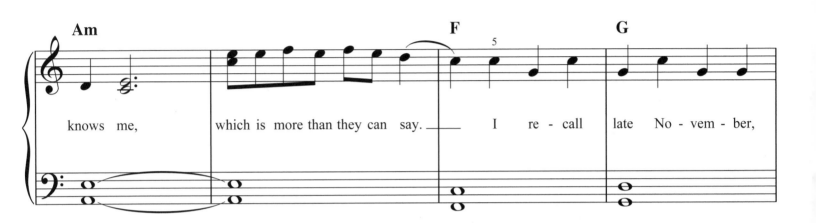

knows me, which is more than they can say. I re-call late No-vem-ber,

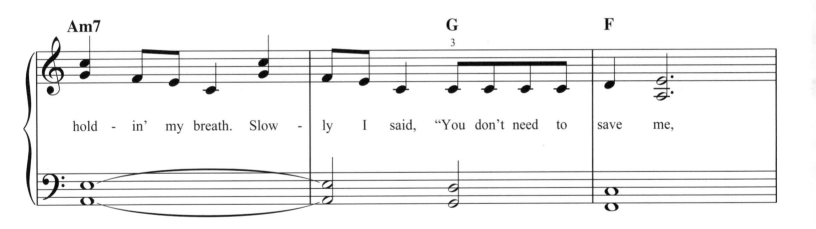

hold-in' my breath. Slow-ly I said, "You don't need to save me,

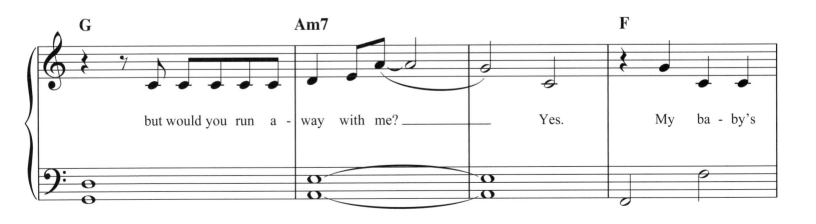

but would you run a-way with me? Yes. My ba-by's

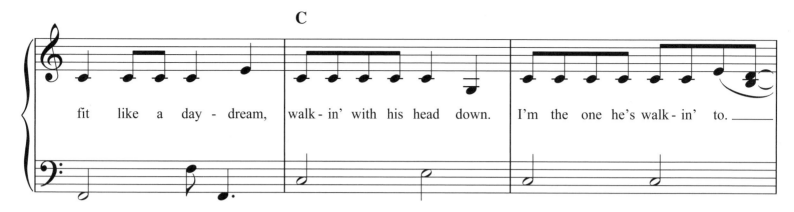

F/A   Am7

So call it what you want, yeah, call it what you want to.

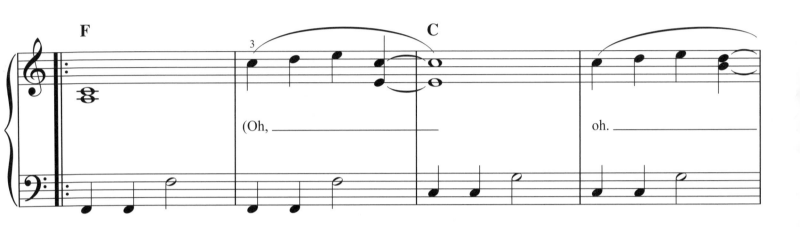

F   C

(Oh, _____   oh. _____

G   1. F/A   Am7

_____   Call it what you want.)

2. F/A   Am   N.C.

Call it what you want, yeah, call it what you want   to.